The Kansas City Investigation

The Kansas City Investigation

Pendergast's Downfall
1938–1939

Rudolph H. Hartmann

Edited with an Introduction by
Robert H. Ferrell

University of Missouri Press
Columbia and London

Library of Congress Cataloging-in-Publication Data

Hartmann, Rudolph H.
   The Kansas City investigation : Pendergast's downfall, 1938–1939 /
Rudolph H. Hartmann ; edited by Robert H. Ferrell.
      p.   cm.
   Includes bibliographical references and index.
   ISBN 0-8262-1231-X
   1. Kansas City (Mo.)—Politics and government.   2. Pendergast,
Tom, 1870–1945.   3. Political corruption—Missouri—Kansas City—
History—20th century.   I. Ferrell, Robert H.   II. Title.
F474.K257H37   1999
978.1'39032—dc21   99-18273
                                                                          CIP

Designer: Stephanie Foley
Typesetter: Crane Composition, Inc.
Printer and binder: Edwards Brothers, Inc.
Typefaces: Bembo and Palatino

Contents

Acknowledgments

The present book by Rudolph H. Hartmann required much assistance, for which I am grateful to Thomas F. Eagleton, Louis C. Gualdoni, Sr., William P. Hannegan, John K. Hulston, Crosby Kemper III, Sara and Gene McKibben, Mickey McTague, Brent Schondelmeyer, and Lee Williams. Carolyn and Donald Hartmann, Sr., can be justifiably proud of the book, in memory of the quiet, modest man they knew a generation and more ago. For assistance in the Franklin D. Roosevelt Library, I am indebted to Lynn Bassanese, Mark Renovitch, Nancy Snedeker, Raymond Teichman, Alycia Vivona, and especially Robert Parks (as mentioned in the Introduction). And thanks to friends in the Harry S. Truman Library: Dennis Bilger, Carol Briley, Ray Geselbracht, Elizabeth Safly, Randy Sowell, and Pauline Testerman. Again it is a pleasure to work with Beverly Jarrett, director and editor-in-chief of the University of Missouri Press; Jane Lago, who is managing editor; and the editor who put it all together, John Brenner. A thank-you, once more, to Lila and Carolyn.

A Note on the Editing

The author of *The Kansas City Investigation* wrote clearly and in orderly fashion, as one would have expected of the chief investigator of the Intelligence Unit, and so the task of an editor was not difficult. The only changes in Hartmann's original manuscript are minor. In addition to a few typos and misspellings and grammatical errors, there were small redundancies, such as listing the states of cities, such as "Kansas City, Missouri." The author wrote "Mr." in front of proper names, and that mark of courtesy is gone. He was fond of capitalizing, and with few exceptions government departments, bureaus, and units are in lower case. Numbers to 101 are written out, and similarly all even numbers. With the above exceptions, and changes in a few commas, the manuscript of 1942 appears as its author wrote it.

The Kansas City Investigation

Introduction

THE SEARCH ROOM of the Franklin D. Roosevelt Library in Hyde Park, New York, is an unlikely place to discover an absolutely first-rate, book-length manuscript. The more so because it was in the papers of a well-known figure in the Roosevelt administration, Secretary of the Treasury Henry Morgenthau, Jr. Fifty years and more have passed since research in the Roosevelt Library began, during which eager doctoral students and their professorial teachers have searched the papers of the president and his cabinet officers and other administration officials too numerous to mention. What more possibly could be left to find? In recent years the scholars have gone to other presidential libraries (of which the FDR Library was the first), to West Branch, Independence, Abilene, Boston, Austin, Ann Arbor, Atlanta, Simi Valley, College Station. There they make their discoveries, and place them appropriately in their articles and books.

The search room itself testifies to the unlikelihood of finding anything new in the Roosevelt Library. Researchers once were directed to a sumptuous room to the right of the building's entrance, paneled, replete with varnished tables and upholstered chairs, everything marking the importance of research. Now it is upstairs in an alcove, and a researcher must pass through a virtually unmarked door, walk up an iron stairway, make two or three abrupt turns, and pass into a modestly appointed room.

Most of the library building has been turned into a museum. A handsome edifice made of field stone, to which wings were added, it was dedicated in 1941. It stands perhaps an eighth of a mile off the Albany Post Road, otherwise known as Route 10, and is approached or departed from by two lanes bordered by carefully

1

trimmed young trees. The library museum has gathered a vast array of memorabilia concerning Roosevelt's presidency. Outside is a bronze bust of the president, affixed to a pedestal. Inside are the paintings and prints and ship models and photographs and newspapers celebrating Roosevelt's time in American history. Downstairs is the president's specially designed automobile that he drove himself, with hand-held substitutes for foot pedals. Next to the car is the bookstore and gift shop. Tourists old and young, with or mostly without memory of the Roosevelt era, throng the exhibit rooms and close their visits with trips downstairs to see the automobile and purchase postcards.

If the library now appears much diminished in a scholarly way, confirmation of that fact lies in its surroundings. The nineteenth-century rambling mansion still stands to the north of the library building, the house that the late historian of Roosevelt, Frank Freidel, described as unpretentious. That might be true, compared (as Freidel did) with the Vanderbilt mansion nearby. For most tourists it is impressively unpretentious. But everywhere else is the modernity, so one might describe it, that almost presses upon and surely diminishes the past. Coming back again and again to a library I have seen since the early 1950s, I am forced constantly to compare the new and the old, for the Roosevelt Library and the house almost inevitably focus attention on the veritable trashing of the lower Hudson Valley that has taken place since the president's death in 1945. The library and house seem strangely out of place. Doubtless some of the trashing occurred before President Roosevelt passed on; he must have seen some of it. Whatever, the old lies west of the Post Road and the library's and mansion's stone fence. The new is on the east side, stretching south to Poughkeepsie, north to the village of Hyde Park and on up through Rhinebeck. All along the east side can be seen the all-American collection of enterprises, beer places and health centers and a down-at-the-screen outdoor movie and a shopping center that boasts the locality's principal supermarket together with the latest arrangement of what once was known as a drugstore. My concern late in August of 1998, a poor time to frequent Hyde Park, it turned out, was the county fair, which filled the motels with roustabouts, as well as with tourists swarming to visit the presidential center, that is, the museum. My first stop in a sort of motel odyssey was the Roosevelt Inn, a spotless place with paper walls, and after two nights of unwanted conversation and television I shifted to Super-8, much better but chock-full after three days, and thence to the Golden Manor, the huge neon sign of which acts as a moon reflecting directly across the Post Road and the stone wall to the Roosevelt house itself. If President Roosevelt's mother, the redoubtable Sara, who lived until 1941 and published a book entitled *My Boy Franklin,* could look out now and see the Golden Manor's sign, she would have conniption fits.

And so, secure in a feeling that nothing of moment would turn up, that I would discover a few useful details for a book entitled *Truman and Pendergast,* I went ahead with my researches. I was looking for some account of relations between President Roosevelt and Boss Tom Pendergast of Kansas City, Missouri. The two were not altogether dissimilar individuals. Pendergast stood 5'9" and weighed 245 pounds. Balding, with small, sharp eyes and a large nose, smooth-shaven, with thick neck and big arms and hands, he showed himself the fighter he once was. During his years as a political boss he had not entirely given up fighting. He was still capable of knocking an opponent through a plate-glass door, and early in the Roosevelt presidency appears to have done so when a visitor to his office unfortunately said the wrong thing. As for the president, he would have liked to be a fighter like Pendergast, but because of his bout with poliomyelitis in 1921 he no longer managed the strength, and confined his fighting to political ways, in which his intricate maneuvering, his admirable footwork, was well known.

For a while during the Roosevelt administration the two men, Pendergast and the president, did political business with each other; there were close connections. One of the connections was that in 1932 and 1936, Pendergast voted Kansas City for the president, which by the latter year meant sixty thousand pads—cemetery people and others. The previous year, 1935, the president arranged a quid pro quo through the national administrator of the Works Progress Administration, FDR's close friend Harry L. Hopkins. Upon recommendation of Missouri's two senators, Harry S. Truman and Bennett Champ Clark, Hopkins installed a Pendergast henchman, Matthew S. Murray of Kansas City, as state WPA director, giving the machine sixty to eighty thousand (some figures go over one hundred thousand) jobs to dispense. This was a considerable advantage to the boss of Kansas City in the midst of the Great Depression when a job, any job, was a precious matter for its holder.

I knew that a tip from an official who had resigned his position in the Treasury Department's Bureau of Internal Revenue early in 1938 had persuaded the president to move against Pendergast. The tip was given by a former Missourian, and he spoke to a reporter in Washington of the *Kansas City Star*. The *Star* hated Pendergast, and the reporter telephoned the governor of Missouri, Lloyd C. Stark. Before his election in 1936, Stark had been proprietor of Stark Brothers Nurseries and Orchards Company in Louisiana, Missouri, the nation's largest nursery and purveyor of "Stark Delicious apples." Stark's term, begun in 1937, was limited by Missouri's constitution to four years, a single term. Stark had in mind to acquire the Senate seat of Truman, elected in 1934, who would have to run in the 1940 Democratic primary for reelection. Truman was a member of the Pendergast machine, and if Stark, who had been elected with Pendergast assistance, were to turn against the boss and destroy the machine, he might easily send himself to the Senate in Truman's place.

The tip against Pendergast, given by the resigning bureau official, concerned a massive bribe taken by Pendergast in 1935–1936 from 137 national fire insurance companies operating in Missouri. The state had entered into a long litigation over raising insurance rates, and though the rates went up, the arrangement was for the excess premiums to be impounded. The impounded sums represented a huge sum for that time, $11 million, and the companies desired to acquire them, or most of them; holders of policies were to receive 20 percent. The bribe to Pendergast totaled $440,000, of which he kept the lion's share and awarded smaller sums to two cooperating individuals, including the state commissioner of insurance.

Why the president ordered the Intelligence Unit of the Bureau of Internal Revenue—the unit dealt with income tax evasion—to move against Pendergast was no particular mystery, and when the library truck stood there in the search room on my first day as a researcher I discovered nothing on that score. Early in 1938, receiving his telephone call, Governor Stark journeyed immediately to Washington and virtually forced the president to move against the Kansas City boss. Anything other than a move with alacrity would have allowed Stark to alert reporters to the administration's inaction in the presence of illegality. Too, the president quickly came to see that the governor, rather than Pendergast, might control Missouri's electoral votes in 1940; the president already, it seems, was beginning to contemplate that he might run for a third term.

What the library truck offered was something else, of remarkable interest: an account of just exactly what Roosevelt did, through the Intelligence Unit, to bring about the collapse of the Pendergast machine the next year, 1939. In advance of my visit I had asked a long-time archivist, Robert Parks, to survey the library's collections and tell me what to look at. He advised examination of seven boxes in the Morgenthau papers, listed as "Confidential Reports about People," and he pointed out 150 or so pages on Pendergast in boxes 386 and 388. I found two small dossiers, each a few pages, in box 386. As Bob advised, I riffled through box 387—he thought it wise to check all seven boxes. The next box, 388, was labeled for the year 1942, by which time Boss Tom had been indicted, convicted, served a year and a day in the prison hospital at Leavenworth where he suffered from heart trouble, and was spending the remaining years of his life (he died in 1945) in his office at the Ready Mixed Concrete Company, of which he was president.

Opening box 388 of Morgenthau's general file was an exhilarating experience—for here was what the dull researches of days, weeks, and beyond, with evenings in golden manors, offer the historical researcher; here was what makes it all worthwhile. The manuscript was single-spaced typescript, 148 pages, and the blue-ribbon original, not a carbon. It was introduced to someone, presumably Secretary Morgenthau, in a short foreword by Elmer L. Irey, head of the Intelligence Unit. Irey had joined the Treasury Department twenty years before, after World War I, and assisted in the successful prosecution of the Chicago gangster, Alphonse Capone. Capone had appeared impervious to prosecution because his lawyers covered his every, it seemed, illegal track, but Irey had gone after him for income tax evasion. In the 1930s the Intelligence Unit managed the same tactic with a succession of gangsters. At the behest of the president in 1938, Morgenthau asked Irey to investigate Pendergast, whose income was obviously underreported. The resultant investigation brought down the boss of Kansas City, together with a group of Pendergast's assistants, in a scandal that rocked the local citizenry, for most Kansas Citians had had no idea of the extent of the Pendergast machine's illegalities. Local surprise was such that when on April 7, 1939, the U.S. government in the person of the federal attorney for the western district of Missouri, Maurice M.

Milligan, announced Pendergast's indictment, the city's principal newspaper, the *Star*, announced the news in headlines so large that they only compared with the paper's announcement of the declaration of war against Germany on April 6, 1917.

The outline of what happened to Pendergast and his henchmen has long been a matter of record, and does not deserve repetition in the present pages. Suffice it to say that the boss was indicted on Good Friday and pleaded not guilty and was released on bond. When a friend sought to help him with his coat so he could be fingerprinted in the office of the U.S. marshal in Kansas City, Pendergast said to no one in particular, "There's nothing the matter with me. They persecuted Christ on Good Friday, and nailed him to the Cross." Toward the end of the month the federal attorney advanced a second indictment. On May 22 the boss suffered a change of mind, if not of heart, and pleaded guilty to the charges, threw himself on the mercy of the court, and within days was in Leavenworth.

Pendergast's former insurance commissioner, Robert Emmet O'Malley, who in 1939 was director of the Kansas City water department, was served when he came out of a church in Baltimore; he was in the East visiting his son. He followed the boss, as did the director of the police department of Kansas City, the head of the state WPA, and assorted other officials, as well as officers of Pendergast enterprises such as the W. A. Ross Construction Company. The boss's bookkeeper testified against the machine, and on May 1 his abandoned automobile was found on a Missouri River bridge, with books of the Pendergast companies that he had agreed to furnish the grand jury, together with two suicide notes; days later his body washed up downriver. Pendergast's principal associate in the city government, City Manager Henry F. McElroy, white-haired, hot-tempered, who liked to relate how he admired his "old Presbyterian mother," resigned, and it became evident that he had looted the city of millions of dollars. He suffered a heart attack, and, while an indictment was in preparation, he suffered a second attack and died.

Senator Truman observed the Kansas City investigation from faraway Washington, and found himself contemplating a grueling contest for renomination, because Stark declared for his seat almost as soon as the investigation ended. Truman was a former official of Jackson County, the county of Kansas City. He had been eastern judge, that is, county commissioner for the largely rural eastern part of the county centering on the then farm town of Independence (now a Kansas City suburb). For eight years he was presiding judge, elected at large to a three-man court. As the highest county official he managed an honest administration, giving Pendergast patronage but no graft. When the machine was tottering he introduced Pendergast's nephew Jim, whom he had known in the war, to Postmaster General James A. Farley. Truman, surprised when Jim pleaded for political measures to relieve his uncle of the income tax investigation, telephoned Farley and apologized. Truman, in truth, had no idea of what had gone on; he believed that under McElroy, with whom he had served when McElroy was western judge on the court, the city was enjoying an honest administration.

Two questions arise about *The Kansas City Investigation: Pendergast's Downfall, 1938–1939.* One is how such a document could have escaped the notice of historians and political scientists for so long.

Why the manuscript was left unread, what—back then—kept all of its words from the 1940s version of the Internet, is an interesting point. Quite probably the reason was the bulk of the Morgenthau papers. When Roosevelt's secretary of the treasury left office in 1945 he took out truckloads of papers, which he denominated as personal, so much material that there was talk about it, talk of whether he had taken official government papers rather than his own. It is true that scholars went through portions of the papers at the Roosevelt Library and wrote about them. It may also be true that the size of the Morgenthau papers tempted researchers to avoid them or read only parts, in belief that someone else had read the other parts. There were two main divisions of the papers, the first being the Morgenthau diaries, which were not diaries but collections of miscellaneous documents, in chronological order, in 864 "books" of several hundred pages each. Secondly was an enormous general file in 1,187 archival boxes varying in width from three to five inches, in which papers were stacked vertically. In the 1980s a microfilm company filmed the diaries for sale to large libraries. The company produced 250 reels, with 63 for the period 1933–1939, 114 for 1940–1942, and 73 for 1943–1945. The company placed no dates on the containers of individual reels for the diaries, apart from their division into three broad periods. At the beginning of each book of the diaries was a table of contents, and there were three or four books to each reel, but the company did not film the tables of contents by themselves, despite the fact that years ago the tables were gathered together and easily could have been filmed. The company promised an index to the diaries and failed to deliver it, despite the fact that the FDR Library long has had available an index of three-by-five cards, twenty-five drawers of them. As for the second main division of the papers, the general file, the company did not film it. This may have led researchers who used only the film—if they could find their way through it—to believe that they had seen everything in the papers.

Scholars may also have taken easy ways out with the Morgenthau papers. The easiest was to use the three published volumes of selections from the diaries brought together by John M. Blum, *From the Morgenthau Diaries* (1959–1967). Another resort, particularly for anyone desiring to use unpublished documents, was to use Morgenthau's memoranda of conversations with the president, which the film company offered in two reels as the Morgenthau diary. Unfortunately, the memoranda of conversations began on January 16, 1938, and from books of the diaries it is evident that Morgenthau did not always make memos of his conversations.

The other question is what recommends publication of this little book.

The answer in part is that it reads like a "whodunit." The reader catches his breath as he sees how the machine in the person of the boss's older brother James, known as Alderman Jim, took its beginnings in the politics of the city's first ward, later controlled the second ward, and went on from there. Young Tom, born in 1872, took over upon Alderman Jim's death in 1911, and soon revealed far more ability and ambition than his brother ever had shown. In the 1920s, Tom bested his rivals, especially after the introduction of the city manager system in 1926. By the end of the decade he was in control. He exiled his principal rival, Joseph B. Shannon, to the national House of Representatives in 1930. In 1932 a fortunate series of circumstances gave him more advantages, making his machine a power throughout the state. Two years later he nominated and elected Judge Truman to the Senate. In 1935 the machine reached its height of power. The boss was a national figure, with both senators, Truman and Clark, apparently (this was not really true) in his pocket, with influence upon most of the state's thirteen members of the House of Representatives, and with control of the governor,

Stark's predecessor, Guy B. Park, who signed anything Pendergast put before him and among other bounties gave the state insurance department to O'Malley.

Another recommendation for the book is that its author, Rudolph H. Hartmann, was the principal investigator of the Intelligence Unit and in charge of the search into Pendergast's income. Hartmann eventually possessed all the information; as the investigation proceeded he learned the details: his account constitutes an "inside" analysis of what happened.

Lastly, the fall of Pendergast and the machine, set out as if it were a mystery story by the treasury's principal investigator, offers opportunity to measure the machine era in American political history. The fall of the Pendergast machine marked the beginning of the end of the long period of boss dominance, if not rule, in Democratic and Republican politics. Boss control had begun after the Civil War when the corruption of those years caused what the reforming journalist Lincoln Steffens, writing about St. Louis, described as the shame of the cities. After World War II, with consignment of most of the federal, state, and city payrolls to civil service, and a general weakening of party structures if only because increasing numbers of Americans described their political allegiances as nonpartisan or (to use the imprecise word of the late Senator Arthur H. Vandenberg of Michigan) bipartisan, party voting became so unpredictable that the machine era came to an end. In Chicago, Mayor Richard J. Daley's son is presently mayor, which says something about the endurance, in dynastic form, of bossism. But the younger Daley is hardly the possessor of the power of his father.

At the present writing, Kansas City long since has virtually forgotten Boss Tom. Alderman Jim's statue stands in Case Park above the West Bottoms, but the alderman's memory is dim to the point of oblivion. Boss Tom upon his death in January 1945 was buried after a hugely attended mass in Visitation Church, but his grave is seldom visited and his memory is not honored with city statuary. The boss's office at 1908 Main Street, in what was once celebrated as the State Capitol, with the governor's mansion in Jefferson City known as Uncle Tom's Cabin, is in a state of worsening disrepair. Years ago the adjoining Monroe Hotel, in which Pendergast housed his homeless supporters and retired minions, disappeared under the wrecker's ball. The two-story brick building stands by itself, the first floor empty of whatever it housed, the revered upper floor, where governors and senators waited in line together with other suitors and suppliants, similarly empty. It is all that remains of what was the greatest political machine of its time, possibly the greatest in American history.

One

Thomas J. Pendergast and Kansas City prior to 1939

P RIOR TO THE YEAR 1939 the names of Kansas City and Thomas J. Pendergast were linked closely together. Born in St. Joseph, Missouri, in 1872, of parents who had emigrated from Tipperary County, Ireland, Pendergast came to Kansas City in 1892 at the age of twenty. He had graduated from Christian Brothers College High School and then had attended St. Marys College at St. Marys, Kansas, where he took an active part in athletics and, due to parental objection, turned down a contract to play professional baseball.[1]

His brother James Francis was operating several saloons in Kansas City and also had a liquor concession at a nearby racetrack. When Thomas came to the city, he secured a position as cashier in a booth at the racetrack and also kept the books for his brother's saloons. Later, under the patronage of his brother, he obtained an appointment as a deputy constable in the famous first ward of Kansas City, where his schooling on the riverfront taught him that a pair of fists were frequently more persuasive than words. His political strength kept on increasing and in 1911, when his brother James died, he took charge of the political organization which his brother had built. This organization grew to great proportions and, during the years 1932 to 1938, he was considered more powerful in Missouri politics than any man before him.[2]

On January 25, 1911, Thomas Pendergast married Carrie Snyder of Belleville, Illinois. Three children were born of this union, Mrs. W. E. Burnett, Jr., Thomas, Jr., and Aileen. Between the years 1927 and 1929 he erected a palatial residence on Ward Parkway in Kansas City, the cost of this residence and the furnishings exceeding $125,000.[3]

The headquarters from which Pendergast directed all of his political activities was located at 1908 Main Street, an address which became a byword in Missouri politics since it was practically impossible for any candidate for political office to be successful unless he paid a visit to "The Old Man at 1908 Main." Next door to these headquarters stands the Monroe Hotel containing 101 rooms and 60 baths, which Pendergast purchased sometime in 1924 at a cost of $285,000. This hotel gave Pendergast an opportunity to shelter many people gratis, who for the time being at least, were without funds and who in return for these accommodations became new recruits to his organization.

Such a person was E. H. Matheus who at one time had been a captain on a steamboat plying the Missouri River. As the river trade diminished, Matheus began looking for other employment but without success until 1927 when, after he received a night's lodging at the Monroe Hotel, Pendergast took an interest in him. Endowed by nature with a brawny physique, Matheus became the personal secretary of Pendergast. As such, it was his principal duty to decide who, among the numerous daily visitors at 1908 Main Street, would be permitted to see the "boss." Some of these visitors were not the kind that could be convinced by soft words and, in such instances, the brawn of Matheus stood him in good stead in denying an obstreperous visitor the right to enter into the presence of Pendergast. Matheus held this position until 1934 when he became ill. As a reward for his faithful service, he was given free lodging in the Monroe Hotel. His place as secretary was taken by Bernard W. Gnefkow who, besides these duties, was also able to hold a position as chief sanitary inspector for The Sanitary Service Company at $160 per month. The Sanitary Service Company, which collects and disposes of the garbage in Kansas City, was controlled by Pendergast.[4]

Step by step as the political power of Pendergast increased, lawlessness, or rather the unenforcing of the law, increased. Gambling became a major industry, and without any pretense of concealment gambling houses as numerous as drugstores advertised their existence. The underworld flocked to these establishments, where "hostesses," some of them clad in the short skirts of the dance halls of the Old West, induced patrons to play the games or to buy drinks. Saloons also thrived, although few paid the city and state licenses. It was often stated and borne out by the facts that "Kansas City is the widest open town in the U. S. A.—anything goes."

Such conditions attracted the denizens of the underworld, from the petty sneak thief to the machine-gunning gangsters. Fences disposed of stolen property unmolested and, as a result, theft insurance rates were higher in Kansas City than most other cities.

It was impossible for the decent element among the population of Kansas City to do anything about these conditions. The use of the ballot box in electing trustworthy officials was of no avail. The machine did the voting. Honest voters were intimidated and driven from the polls, or if this action did not suffice, the votes not cast as the machine desired were not counted in the final tabulation.[5] The city administration and even the police department was entirely dominated by Pendergast. As city manager he had put in H. F. McElroy, and he named Otto Higgins director of police. Another close friend of Pendergast, Matthew S. Murray, was named director of public works, which office controlled the letting of all contracts for public improvements in Kansas City. The construction companies, headed by J. J. Pryor and Michael Ross, and in which Pendergast had interests, received all the contracts. Outsiders just did not bid, or if they did, threats usually caused them to withdraw the bids, or if they remained adamant their bids were just ignored. Other companies in which Pendergast was interested, more or less, also profited, namely, the Ready Mixed Concrete Company, Kansas City Concrete Pipe Company, Sanitary Service Company, Missouri Contracting Corporation, Centropolis Crusher Company, Midwest Paving Company, Mid-West Pre Cote Company, Missouri Asphalt Products Company, and the Dixie Machinery and Equipment Company. Contracts were not let for public improvements in Kansas City unless one or more of his companies participated. Then Murray was made administrator of the WPA projects without his relinquishing his city position, and the vicious circle was complete. As director of public works for the city, Murray had the authority that went with the inspection power over plumbing, boilers, and smoke, and this authority was used against any opponents of Pendergast's regime.

John Lazia was the dominant figure on the north side of Kansas City, chiefly populated by Italians. He became a close friend and staunch follower of Pendergast and it was rumored that he was the protector of the Kansas City gambling houses. He was often referred to as the unofficial chief of police.

On June 17, 1933, a federal officer, three Kansas City police officers, and Frank Nash, a federal prisoner, were killed by gangsters in an attempt to liberate the prisoner. This massacre took place at the Union Station plaza at Kansas City in broad daylight. A grand jury found that certain Kansas City police officials had instructed their men not to investigate the killings. Lieutenant George Rayen, head of the police motor car theft bureau, was one of the several indicted for perjury. He was alleged to have said, "I am in the employ of Kansas City, Missouri; nevertheless, I owe a greater duty there to the organization which is headed by Mr. Pendergast."

A few months later, namely on August 12, 1933, Charles Gargotta, a close friend of Lazia, with three companions was in the act of shooting to death Ferris J. Anthon, a liquor racketeer, on Armour Boulevard in a fashionable Kansas City apartment house district, when Sheriff Thomas B. Bash, accompanied by his wife, a guest, and a deputy, driving home, surprised them. Sheriff Bash was attacked by Gargotta and his companions. Returning the fire, the sheriff killed two of them, one escaped, and Gargotta, begging for mercy, surrendered. The sheriff disarmed Gargotta and, after labeling the pistol taken from the latter, turned it over to the Kansas City police department for ballistic examination.

At the trial the sheriff identified the pistol as the one he had taken from Gargotta, but when Leonard L. Claiborne, a city detective, took the stand, he contradicted the testimony of the sheriff, testifying that this pistol had been found by him and that he had labeled it. This testimony upset the case completely and Gargotta was acquitted. Later, when Claiborne was tried for perjury, he was quoted as having said he testified falsely at the instance of a man "higher up" (indicated in the testimony as Lazia) who had promised him promotion to the rank of sergeant.

A charge against Gargotta of attempting to murder Sheriff Bash was continued from time to time by County Prosecutor W. W. Graves, who also was a henchman of Pendergast. In December 1938, five years after the crime had been committed and after twenty-eight continuances had been granted, Graves dismissed the charge. Later, after the Pendergast regime began to disintegrate, Governor Lloyd C. Stark demanded that action be taken in this matter, and Gargotta was reindicted and Graves was also indicted for alleged neglect of duty. Graves was later ousted and on June 14, 1939, Gargotta entered a plea of guilty to the assault charge and was sentenced to three years in prison.

Finally, Adam Richetti was indicted by a state grand jury as one of the murderers in the massacre at the Union Station. His associates who were alleged to have aided in the murders, "Pretty Boy" Floyd and Verne C. Miller, had been since slain, Floyd by federal officers in Ohio, and Miller by gangsters near Detroit.

With control of the police, the courts, the prosecutors, and the facility of gangsters to intimidate witnesses, Pendergast's machine was able to operate without fear of any legal action.[6]

During the year 1932, Pendergast was able to disclose that he not only controlled Kansas City but also the State of Missouri, and that he was the power behind the throne. For years Pendergast, who was devoted to horse racing and maintained a stable of race horses, had maintained, if not personally, at least through his influence, a racetrack in Platte County, which is about an hour's drive by automobile from Kansas City. The laws of the State of Missouri forbade horse racing, but the law was never enforced in this county due to the fact that every case taken to court to stop this flouting of the law was either dismissed or otherwise disposed of by a circuit judge in that county by the name of Guy B. Park. In return for this concession to horse racing, Pendergast through his political organization was able to assure the reelection of Park whenever it became necessary.[7]

During the primary election in the year 1932, the voters nominated Francis M. Wilson as Democratic nominee for governor of the State of Missouri. Wilson was the people's choice, but on October 12, 1932, Wilson died, and it was necessary to name someone else to be in the lists as standard-bearer. The Democratic state committee met at Jefferson City for this purpose and quite a few names were mentioned for consideration. The name of Judge Park was placed in nomination, but the majority of the committee members did not approve of this, some contending that Judge Park was not well known to the voters, and others contending that there would be considerable opposition due to the gambling situation in Platte County. However, when Pendergast spoke in favor of Judge Park, the committee decided not to antagonize him and therefore the name of Judge Park was placed on the ballot as nominee for the governorship of Missouri. In the general elections Park was elected governor. He must have felt very devoted to the man who had raised him from an obscure judgeship to governor of the State of Missouri. One of Governor Park's first official actions was to name Robert Emmet O'Malley to the important post of state superintendent of insurance. O'Malley was a very close friend of Pendergast, having been associated with him in the early days of his political career as leader of the first ward in Kansas City.

Two

Conviction of Lazia

JOHN LAZIA, the right-hand man of Pendergast, who it was rumored was the "higher up" directing all the killings, kidnapings, and beatings administered in Kansas City, was closely allied to the owners of the North Side Finance Company and the North Side Distributing Company. This latter company was composed of a partnership of twelve powerful north-side Italians reputed to be gangsters and racketeers.[1] Sugar was furnished exclusively to bootleggers for the manufacture of illicit alcohol and liquor.

During the fall of 1931 revenue agent Harry D. Beach commenced an income tax investigation of these two companies and, as a result, obtained sufficient information to warrant a similar investigation of the income tax liability of Lazia. This information disclosed that the Merchants Bank had issued cashier's checks to Lazia during the years 1929 and 1930 aggregating $50,000, that Lazia spent money freely, and that he was interested in several gambling establishments.

In view of these developments, revenue agent Beach began an investigation. Discovering no income tax returns filed by Lazia for the years 1929 and 1930, he requested him to appear for an interview. On March 9, 1932, Lazia appeared and a conference was held in the offices of the Intelligence Unit, then located in the Federal Reserve Bank Building, which was next door to the Grand Avenue Temple Building. In the last-named building the offices of the revenue agents were located.[2] Lazia was accompanied by Isadore Rich, an attorney, and in addition to Beach the government was represented by special agent in charge David Nolan, revenue agent in charge Charles T. Russell, and special agent Robert L. Sharp. At this

17

conference Lazia admitted that he had received some income during the years in question but that he had gambled extensively and had suffered losses far in excess of his income.

Revenue agent Beach, who was a bachelor, resided at that time at the Berkshire Arms Hotel, in Kansas City. Desiring to share the apartment with some young man, he had placed an advertisement in the Sunday editions of the newspapers on February 28, March 6, and March 13, 1932, as follows:

> Want young man, about 23, to share studio apartment. Linwood-Troost; rent reasonable; references exchanged. Valentine 4944, Apt. 916. Sundays or evenings.

This advertisement did not contain Beach's name or the name of the apartment-hotel.

About 11:30 P.M. Saturday, March 12, 1932, three days after the conference with Lazia, two men, one apparently under the influence of liquor, entered the lobby of the hotel, started for the elevator, then returned and approached the desk, where J. A. Piorer, the night clerk, was on duty. One of the men stated that he desired to see "Beach" in apartment no. 906, to which Piorer replied that Beach was occupying apartment no. 916, not 906. This information appeared to bother or perplex them. One of the visitors then requested the night clerk to call Beach and tell him that "Frank" was in the lobby. Although the night clerk knew that Beach was in and had been since about 10:45 P.M., he informed the visitors that Beach was not in his apartment. The two men, after a few whispered comments, which could not be understood, departed. Beach was known for the quiet, secluded life he led, and the night clerk felt certain that Beach would not want to be disturbed.

About 2:15 P.M. the following day two men, answering the descriptions of the two men who called the evening before, came to Beach's apartment and asked whether he had advertised for someone to share the apartment. Beach replied that he had and invited them to enter. He was curious as to how they had discovered the apartment, because in the advertisement he had neither given his nor the apartment's name, but the strangers did not give him any satisfactory answer. After inspecting the apartment, both men stated they were unemployed and their conversation was very vague as to their present addresses and previous occupations.

Beach realized immediately that neither one of these men would be desirable for sharing the apartment and wanted to close the interview as soon as possible. Answering their questions, he told them he was an accountant and was employed in the Grand Avenue Temple Building, but refrained from telling them the name of his employer. As soon as he had mentioned the name of the building in which he was employed, both men arose and went to the door as if to depart. However, they hesitated at the door and one of them requested a drink of water. The kitchenette being but a few steps from the door, Beach went there to get them the water, and overheard one of the men say, "He is the one we want." Immediately thereafter he was struck in the jaw by the fist of one of the men, the blow knocking him to the floor, and both of them proceeded to kick and beat him. Fortunately he was able to protect the upper portion of his head sufficiently to avoid being killed by the kicks and blows. His cries for help went unheeded and finally the two men, believing Beach dead, departed, closing the door after them. They fled down the stairs from the ninth to the second floor, leaped from the second story window, and escaped. Several persons saw them in their flight, but, although they were able to furnish good descriptions and although many suspects were arrested and questioned, the assailants were never apprehended.

In the meantime Beach was able to reach the telephone in his room and notify the clerk of his condition. He was removed to St. Mary's Hospital in a critical condition. His jaw was fractured in several places and the skull behind the right ear had also been fractured. Although Beach returned to duty after several months, during which time several operations were performed on his broken jaw, he never recovered from this experience and September 24, 1936, he died. Death was partially due to the fact that he was not able to use his jaws sufficiently to eat and had to subsist chiefly on liquid foods.

Robbery certainly was not a motive because no money or jewelry in the room was taken, and the private life of Beach was such that he had no social enemies. There is no doubt but that it was planned to put Beach away, because his activities in investigating the gangster element of the north side of Kansas City were becoming obnoxious to them. He had defied the machine and the machine had answered.

Revenue agent Harry T. Riley was assigned to take over the

unfinished task of investigating the income tax liability of Lazia. With special agent Sharp he proceeded to fulfill this task. Almost insurmountable obstacles had to be overcome. Witnesses who had paid money to Lazia were afraid to give testimony for fear the gangster element would take revenge on them and, since even the police were dominated by the machine, there was little if any protection that could be afforded them.[3] Even high bank officials were reluctant to say anything which might displease the "higher-ups."

However, by laborious and painstaking investigation, the treasury agents slowly began to develop evidence that Lazia did have sufficient income upon which tax should have been paid. It was found that he owned a greyhound racetrack in Clay County near Kansas City and a gambling resort known as the Cuban Gardens.[4] These properties were leased to individuals who operated them, paying rent for this privilege. To cover up the actual ownership the deeds to these properties were carried in the names of employees of the Merchants Bank. The rents were collected by Raymond A. Edlund, cashier of that bank, who although denying that he knew the real owner of these two pieces of property admitted that the $6,000 per annum he collected as rents was delivered or credited by him to Lazia.

It was further discovered that Lazia owned stock in the Duke Motor Company, although the stock certificates were carried in the names of persons who, when interviewed, stated they did not own any of this stock. Edlund, whose name appeared on one of these stock certificates and who apparently had often acted as agent for Lazia, admitted that Lazia had used these stock certificates as collateral on a loan at the Merchants Bank, that he had endorsed the dividend checks for Lazia and had credited these dividends, aggregating $2,160, to the loan account of Lazia.

These witnesses were not eager to testify, and several admitted that they feared reprisals. Finally, sufficient evidence of income had been secured to indicate that Lazia should have filed income tax returns for the years 1929 and 1930 and that he should have paid a tax thereon.

The evidence accumulated by the treasury agents disclosed that for the year 1929, Lazia had a net income of $82,042.25 on which he should have paid a tax of $11,167.84, and that for the year 1930 he had a net income of $98,290.83 upon which a tax of $15,741.17 was due.[5]

On March 11, 1933, the treasury agents were instructed to present the evidence to U.S. Attorney William L. Vandeventer at Kansas City. Since no grand jury was in session and since prosecution for the year 1929 would be barred by the statute of limitations, insofar as failure to file was concerned on March 15, 1933, Vandeventer filed a criminal information on March 14, 1933, against Lazia charging him with intentional failure to file an income tax return for the year 1929.[6] Further action was to depend on what a grand jury would do when the evidence was presented to it. The next grand jury for that district was not to be called until September 1933.

Lazia apparently had no fear that actual prosecution would be undertaken. It was practically certain that Pendergast would endeavor to do something to protect his chief lieutenant and mainstay in north Kansas City, although about this time it was noticed that Charles V. Carrollo, who for several years had aided Lazia in controlling this section of the city, was gaining in power. But Pendergast was doing something.

On November 30, 1934, in a copyrighted article, the *St. Louis Post-Dispatch* disclosed that the following letter had been sent by Pendergast:

May 12, 1933

James A. Farley
Postmaster-General
Washington, D.C.

Dear Jim:

Jerome Walsh and John Lazia will be in Washington to see you about the same matter that I had Mr. Kemper talk to you about. Now, Jim, Lazia is one of my chief lieutenants and I am more sincerely interested in his welfare than anything you might be able to do for me now or in the future. He has been in trouble with the Income Tax Department for some time. I know it was simply a case of being jobbed because of his Democratic activities. I think that Frank Walsh spoke to the proper authorities about this. In any event, I wish you would use your utmost endeavor to bring about a settlement of this matter. I cannot make it any stronger, except to say that my interest in him is greater than anything that might come up in the future.

Thanking you for any and everything you can do, I remain,

Sincerely, your friend,
T. J. Pendergast

After the criminal information had been filed, Lazia employed Jerome Walsh, a Kansas City attorney, and the latter's father, Frank P. Walsh, a nationally known New York lawyer.[7] During the summer of 1933 several conferences were held between Lazia and his attorneys and officials of the government. The defense attorneys demanded that the treasury agents be removed from the case, stating that they were prejudiced, but this demand was denied. While these conferences were pending, U.S. Attorney Vandeventer was advised not to present the case to the grand jury.

When the grand jury was called in September 1933, Vandeventer had not received instructions to present the case, and when the grand jury informed Federal Judge Merrill E. Otis that they desired to investigate the Lazia case, he informed the court of this fact. Judge Otis advised the grand jury that they did not have to await instructions and suggested they proceed with the investigation. At the same time Vandeventer received instructions from the attorney general to present the case, since examination of all the evidence presented at the conferences had failed to disclose anything which would justify further delay.

On September 16, 1933, the grand jury indicted Lazia, charging him with willful failure to file an income tax return for the year 1930 and with evasion of income taxes for the years 1929 and 1930. The case was set for trial on December 18, 1933. Frank P. Walsh then filed an affidavit with the court that he could not prepare the case for trial on that date and also filed a motion for a bill of particulars. Judge Otis granted a continuance to February 5, 1934, and directed that the defendant be furnished with a bill of particulars, which was done on December 27, 1933.

Meanwhile, the term of office of Vandeventer expired January 31, 1934, and Maurice M. Milligan was under consideration for the position.[8] However, since Vandeventer was familiar with all of the aspects of the case, he was appointed as special assistant attorney general to continue to prosecute this case.

Several other moves were made on the part of the defense to gain another continuance, all of which were denied by Judge Otis, and the case went to trial on February 5, 1934. Frank Walsh, renowned through the United States as one of the best criminal defense attorneys, exerted all of his skill, while Vandeventer, with his customary precision, systematically presented the evidence. The case was fiercely contested. Treasury agents Nolan, Sharp, Beach, and Riley were on the witness stand three days, of which two days were consumed in a bitter cross-examination.

Outside the influences were also at work to intimidate the jury. Whenever the jury was taken to the Pickwick Hotel for meals, automobiles filled with Italians would cruise slowly down the street alongside the walking jurymen and, although no verbal remarks were made, sufficient signs were made to leave an impression on them that they were being pointed out and discussed.

On one instance, near the close of the trial, while the jury was returning to the Federal Building, a youth with only one newspaper under his arm ran past the jurymen shouting, "Extra! Extra! Jury does its duty and acquits Lazia."

With the conditions as they were in Kansas City, with the lawless element protected, it is not difficult to realize the impressions such incidents were likely to make on the minds of the jurymen.

At 4:30 P.M. on February 13, 1934, the trial was completed and the case was given to the jury. The jury deliberated until 2:30 P.M. the following day, when they returned a verdict of guilty with respect to willful failure to file income tax returns for the years 1929 and 1930 and a verdict of not guilty with respect to evasion of income taxes for those years. On February 28, 1934, Judge Otis sentenced Lazia to serve twelve months in the Christian County jail at Ozark, Missouri, and to pay a fine of $2,500 on the first count and to serve twelve months in the Gentry County jail at Albany, and to a fine of $2,500 on the second count. The prison sentence and the fine on the second count were suspended, and instead he was placed on probation for five years to begin after the term on the first count had been served. Lazia filed a petition for an appeal and he was released on a $5,000 supersedeas bond.[9]

It was true the government had failed to convict Lazia on the felony counts and had to satisfy itself with conviction on the two misdemeanor counts, but the first attack had been made on the machine, and under the circumstances, much had been accomplished.

Lazia's appeal was never heard by the circuit court of appeals. On July 10, 1934, while free on bond, Lazia was shot at 3:00 A.M. by two men who ambushed him while he was entering the Park Central Hotel where he resided with his wife. With him at the time was Charles Carrollo. As Lazia stepped from his automobile he was met by a blaze of gunfire. He was taken to St. Joseph Hospital, where it was found that eight bullets had entered his body, one piercing his right lung. He died on July 11, 1934.[10]

Since Lazia was a member of the machine, the police department, which had done little in the Union Station massacre, went into action. Every detective on the force was assigned to find the assassins of Lazia, but although many suspects were arrested, no one was ever brought to trial. In his place as leader of the north side came another ruthless person, Charles Carrollo.

Three

Further Developments in Kansas City

LAZIA WAS DEAD, but the machine kept on functioning. Carrollo now became Pendergast's right-hand man. He was born in Italy in 1902 and entered the United States in 1906. The new world was good to him, especially Kansas City. Under Lazia he had conducted several gambling establishments. Now with Lazia gone, he not only kept on with his gambling ventures, but also became the protector of other gamblers, collecting for this protection a tribute, sometimes referred to as a "lug."

In 1936, Pendergast and his wife made a trip to Europe, returning on the maiden voyage of the *Queen Mary* about June 1.[1] He attended the Democratic national convention held at Philadelphia that year, and while at the convention was stricken with a coronary thrombosis. He was critically ill for some time in a hospital in New York. After recovering from the heart attack, Pendergast was beset by abscesses of the lower colon, necessitating the insertion of a drain from the colon from a point above the abscesses to the right side of his abdomen near the hip. This condition would exist for the balance of his life.

He returned to Kansas City in October 1936, the trip from New York being made by a specially chartered train, and upon arrival remained at the Menorah Hospital until November.[2]

On February 2, 1934, just as the trial of Lazia was ready to start, Maurice M. Milligan, of Richmond, Missouri, was sworn in as U.S. attorney in the western district of Missouri. He was later to bear an important part in the disintegration of the Pendergast regime.

The national elections of November 1936 in Kansas City were handled in the same manner as previous ones. Intimidation, altering of votes, and "ghost voters" made the election a farce. Two

25

wards cast more votes than, in the 1930 census, they had inhabitants of all ages.[3]

Milligan started an investigation. The federal grand jury returned scores of indictments against election judges and clerks. As a result of these indictments, 63 persons were convicted by jury trials, 36 persons entered pleas of guilty, and 160 persons entered pleas of nolo contendere. The courts sentenced 34 persons to the penitentiary, 44 persons to jails, and collected fines amounting to $60,000. But although there were indications that these election judges and clerks had committed their crimes at the direction of the machine leaders, evidence to prove that the leaders were involved could not be obtained.

In 1936, Lloyd C. Stark, a prominent businessman of Louisiana, Missouri, who was head of the Stark Brothers Nurseries, famous for their apple trees, was elected governor of Missouri with the consent of Pendergast, succeeding Governor Park. Governor Stark was made of sterner stuff than his predecessor, and almost immediately after moving into the governor's mansion at Jefferson City began doing things as he thought they should be done, without regard to the mandates of Pendergast. On October 19, 1937, he ousted R. E. O'Malley, Pendergast's closest friend, from his position as state superintendent of insurance. Pendergast became furious at this dismissal and was quoted as saying about Governor Stark's future, "I now say, let the river take its course." O'Malley was immediately named director of the Kansas City water department.[4]

Governor Stark claimed he had asked for O'Malley's resignation due to the manner in which the latter had compromised the Missouri fire insurance rate litigation.

Four

Compromise of Impounded Fire Insurance Premiums

O N JANUARY 3, 1928, the U.S. Supreme Court upheld a decision made by the supreme court of Missouri, which decision was that the superintendent of insurance of the State of Missouri had sufficient constitutional power to force fire insurance companies operating in the State of Missouri to a reduction in the rates of premiums. A reduction of 10 percent in rates had been ordered by the superintendent of insurance on October 9, 1922.

Hardly had the aforementioned litigation been decided by the courts when on December 30, 1929, the fire insurance companies filed notice with the superintendent of insurance, who at that time was Joseph B. Thompson, that they intended to increase their rates 16 2/3 percent. This increase was denied them. Suits were filed by 137 fire insurance companies in the U.S. district court, Kansas City, and they obtained injunctions preventing any interference in the collection of the increased rates. At the time these suits were filed, the court ordered that that portion of each premium representing the disputed 16 2/3 percent increase would be impounded until final settlement of the controversy. W. T. Kemper of Kansas City was appointed as custodian of the impounded funds.[1]

The litigation dragged on through the courts. Paul V. Barnett of Kansas City, who had been appointed by the federal court as special commissioner, reported to a three-judge federal court consisting of Circuit Judge Kimbrough Stone and District Judges Albert L. Reeves and Merrill E. Otis. A special commissioner's report disclosed that an increase in rates was justified, but it did not make any recommendation as to the amount of increase. In view of the fact that the State of Missouri had previously won their suit before the Supreme Court of the United States, it was apparent that R. E. O'Malley, the close friend of Pendergast who had been appointed superintendent of insurance in 1933 by Governor Park, would continue the litigation and appeal to the higher courts if a decision adverse to the state were rendered.

R. J. Folonie, an attorney of Chicago, represented the fire insurance companies in this litigation, but the real leader was Charles R. Street, vice-president of the Great American Insurance Company of New York and affiliated insurance companies and in charge of the Chicago branch office, which was also headquarters for the western portion of the United States.[2] Street also was chairman of the Subscribers Actuarial Committee, a committee which was composed of the officers of the leading fire insurance companies to govern the activities of the various companies, the rates charged, and to take care of all matters which affected the companies in common in the western territory. Street was of a strong personality and a masterful leader in the fire insurance business. Aided by his position as chairman of the aforementioned committee, he wielded a tremendous power over the actions of the fire insurance companies and practically dominated all their affairs in the western territory. He was born in Mississippi of an aristocratic family, was married, and had one child, Donald M. Street, who was employed in the investment department of the Guarantee Trust Company, New York.

Street virtually had dictatorial powers over all of the fire insurance companies and decided who the officers of the various companies would be. If he had a grievance against any candidate for an office in another company, he was able to exert enough pressure through his position as chairman of the Subscribers Actuarial Committee to keep the candidate from becoming an officer. He was extremely arrogant in his manner and several other committee members stated that, when someone on the committee had the temerity to request Street to account in any manner for monies entrusted to him, Street would angrily ask whether the committee member making the request believed that he was dishonest. This action would usually result in the committee assuring Street that they did not believe he was dishonest, and no further request for any accounting would be made. Another anecdote has been told about Street, that while attending a session of fire insurance executives, numerous speeches had been held praising the cooperation of the officers of the various companies. Toward the close of the session Street was called upon to say a few words. Upon arising from his chair he said, "In all of the speeches that I have heard today, co-operation has been stressed, but in my opinion the only man who I can say cooperates is the one who does my bidding or does as I want him to." Street was also considered to be miserly, and the story is told that when he would leave his office in inclement weather, although close to seventy years of age, he would cross Michigan Avenue, with all of its traffic, in order to take a taxicab on the east side of the street going north so that he would avoid an additional charge caused by the taxicab having to go a few extra blocks south before being able to make a turn.

Street was anxious to settle the Missouri rate cases. He was getting old, and it was his chief hope that he could settle these rate cases before his death. Furthermore, the fire insurance companies were losing quite a bit of business to new companies which had entered the field and which were obeying the order of the superintendent of insurance for reduction in premiums. He therefore was ready and willing to accept any plan which might avoid long litigation which would result, even if victory were won in the lower courts, before final victory was accomplished in the Supreme Court. Folonie, on the other hand, had no desire to settle the case in any manner, because he felt that ultimate victory would be won in the courts and that the fire insurance companies would not have to make any concessions.

Street on account of his mannerisms and personality had very few friends. One close friend, however, was Alphonsus Logouri McCormack of St. Louis. McCormack was an insurance man and vice-president of the Fire Underwriters Association and president of the Missouri Association of Insurance Agents. McCormack was married in 1909 and has two daughters, Patricia and Louise. He and his wife separated September 1, 1928, and were divorced a year later, but in November 1935 they remarried. He studied law at St. Louis University, graduating in 1926, and was admitted to the bar the same year. Due to his activities in the fire insurance business, and as head of the Missouri Association of Insurance Agents, McCormack was vitally interested in the rate litigation. Commissions earned by the agents on the 16 2/3 percent excess collected were contained in the funds impounded by the court, and he was naturally desirous of having these funds released in order that he and the agents would receive their commissions.

In May 1935, the total excess premiums impounded by the federal court in Kansas City amounted to $9,020,279.01. This large fund lying there idle was a prize that both the fire insurance companies and the superintendent of insurance were eagerly expecting to receive.[3]

On May 14, 1936, Street journeyed to Kansas City, where he met O'Malley, superintendent of insurance. The conference was also attended by Folonie, J. T. Barker of Kansas City representing the state's attorney, P. W. Terry of St. Louis representing the Missouri inspection bureau, P. B. McHaney, chief counsel for the insurance department, and McCormack. At this conference a compromise settlement was agreed upon whereby the impounded premiums would be divided as follows: 50 percent to be paid direct to the fire insurance companies; 30 percent to be set aside in a trust fund with Street and Folonie as trustees; and 20 percent to be distributed to the policy holders. Out of the 30 percent trust fund the Missouri insurance department was to receive $200,000 as reimbursement for expenses, the state's attorneys would be paid their fees, and after the insurance companies' attorneys had received their fees and after the payment of incidental expenses of litigation, the balance left in the trust fund was to be distributed to the companies. On May 18, 1935, the aforementioned stipulation of settlement was signed by O'Malley and Street. When it was delivered to Governor Park for his approval the governor conferred with Roy McKittrick, attorney general of the State of Missouri. McKittrick informed the governor that he did not believe the compromise was legal and in correct form and advised the governor not to approve it. The governor agreed to this disapproval, stating that since he was an attorney himself he could see flaws in the document. Park then returned to the governor's mansion and two hours later signed and approved the compromise, later admitting that, after he had returned to the mansion, he had communicated by telephone with Thomas Pendergast of Kansas City.

The offer in compromise was presented to the three-judge federal court of Kansas City, where it was held pending action by any intervenor. Street had a clause inserted in the compromise agreement that no accounting of this 30 percent fund could be demanded. Later the court upon approving the settlement altered this clause to read that no accounting of this trust fund could be required unless the court desired an accounting.

On February 1, 1936, the three-judge court approved the compromise, and Kemper, the custodian, was ordered to disburse the impounded premiums as directed by the stipulation. There were immediate protests by all the newspapers in Missouri due to the fact that, although in a previous case the state had been upheld in a reduction of rates of premiums, the superintendent of insurance had compromised this new case, agreeing that the policyholders should only receive 20 percent of the impounded premiums. This also caused Governor Stark to oust O'Malley.[4] There were many allegations made that someone had profited by this compromise settlement, but no one knew who this person was, and the mystery of the 30 percent trust fund that had been created gave rise to much speculation, especially in view of the fact that Street had suggested that no accounting be made of this trust fund.

Five

Developments prior to Investigation

FOR SEVERAL YEARS Ernest H. Hicks was a member of the law firm of Hicks and Folonie. Hicks died on October 2, 1935. The following year a revenue agent was assigned to verify the income tax return of Hicks for the period prior to the latter's death. In examining the books of the partnership, Hicks and Folonie, he discovered that on May 9, 1935, the partnership had received $100,500, which had been immediately disbursed. Further investigation disclosed that this receipt of money consisted of fourteen checks from certain fire insurance companies and that the disbursement had been made by two $50,000 checks and one $500 check, payable to Charles R. Street. The revenue agent interviewed Folonie with respect to this receipt and disbursement of $100,500. Folonie stated that the fire insurance companies had issued these checks payable to Hicks and Folonie but that this money belonged to Street, who was taking care of the Missouri rate litigation, and that this money did not represent income to the firm of Hicks and Folonie. In fact Folonie stated that the only reason the receipt and disbursement had been made through the partnership account had been for the convenience of Street. The revenue agent then interviewed Street. The latter furnished the revenue agent with a signed statement admitting the receipt of $100,500 and stating that this money was not income to Hicks and Folonie. He, however, would not give any information as to what the money represented or what disposition had been made of it. Since Street was absent from Chicago most of the time in connection with his varied duties, it was difficult for the revenue agent to contact him. However, several interviews were held with Street at various times, and at these interviews Street denied that this $100,500 was income to him and on several occasions intimated that someone else had received the money. On one occasion he even intimated that a politician had received the money. He however steadfastly refused to divulge the name of the alleged recipient. On May 4, 1936, Street wrote a letter to the revenue agent, stating as follows:

> Leaving for South Dakota. On my return next week will take a run to Mo.—Going to St. Louis on business anyway—and see what they have to say. Don't think can do anything at least before the *Queen Mary* comes in.
>
> C. R. Street

The passenger list of the *Queen Mary*, which made its maiden run from Liverpool to New York about this time, disclosed that among the passengers aboard the ship were Mr. and Mrs. Thomas J. Pendergast. On July 24, 1936, Street wrote another letter to the revenue agent, stating therein:

> My Missouri party phoned. He is tied up with a Democratic primary on August 4 and cannot come up or see me until that is over. Am leaving for 10 days' rest but will be back August 3 and in Mo. a few days later.
>
> C. R. Street

On March 7, 1937, a summons was issued on Street for him to appear before the revenue agent and to give testimony with respect to the $100,500. He appeared with his attorney on March 8, 1937, and refused to answer any questions on the ground that his answers might tend to incriminate him. He also announced that he had filed an amended return that same date for the year 1935, including therein the $100,500 as other income and had paid additional taxes of $47,093.08 plus interest of $2,825.60.

In view of the fact that it was rumored that the "payoff" in the fire insurance rate litigation settlement had been closer to $500,000 than $100,000 and, since Street had temporarily blocked further investigation by reporting the $100,500 and refusing to testify, it was believed advisable to await the filing of an income tax return of Street for the year 1936. If it were true that the payoff had been closer to $500,000 than $100,000, it was felt certain that Street would not be able to report such a large sum of money as income and pay the tax thereon in the following year.[1]

On January 25, 1938, Street went to the hospital in Chicago for examination, where it was disclosed that he was suffering from cancer, and, after an operation, died on February 1, 1938. His death complicated the entire matter because now his lips had been sealed forever in giving testimony as to who had received the payoff.[2]

Six

Investigation of the Activities of Charles R. Street

AFTER STREET'S DEATH the case was assigned to the
Intelligence Unit, Bureau of Internal Revenue, for investigation. Three treasury agents, special agent R. H. Hartmann and revenue agents L. B. Sullivan and P. J. McGrath, were
called to Washington and assigned to the case. To lay the ground-
work for the investigation, the treasury agents went to Kansas City
and examined the records of Kemper, in whose custody the impounded premiums had been held, and discovered that Kemper
had made the distribution in accordance with the stipulation approved by the court, namely, he had sent 50 percent, or $4.5 million,
to the insurance companies; 30 percent, or $2.7 million, to Street
and Folonie to be held in trust, and was reimbursing $1.8 million to
the policyholders.

While the agents were thus engaged, Governor Stark and U.S.
Attorney Milligan journeyed to Washington, their object being to
furnish the government with information concerning the alleged
payoff in the fire insurance rate compromise. They conferred with
Harold N. Graves, assistant secretary of the treasury, who after
hearing their story requested that the treasury agents assigned to
the case be called to Washington for a conference. This was done,
and at the conference the governor and Milligan, after repeating the
allegations that in their opinion a payoff had been made to Pendergast, offered the facilities of their offices to the agents. This offer
was accepted by Graves.[1]

The treasury agents then went to Chicago and audited the records
of the mysterious trust fund, which were now in the custody of the
remaining trustee, R. J. Folonie. This audit disclosed that the trust
fund paid, according to stipulation, the expenses of the Missouri

35

insurance department, the fees of attorneys employed by the state, and the fees of attorneys of the fire insurance companies. It was further disclosed that on March 9, 1936, a month after the court had approved the settlement, an amount equal to 11 percent of the total impounded premiums had been paid to the insurance companies, and on December 24, 1937, an amount equivalent to 5 percent of the impounded premiums likewise had been paid to these companies. These payments were in accordance with the stipulation that any funds remaining after the payment of expenses would be paid to the fire insurance companies. However, an interesting fact was noted with respect to the payment on March 9, 1936. Instead of preparing one check for each of the 137 fire insurance companies involved for 11 percent of the total impounded premiums, it was disclosed that two checks had been prepared for each company, one equivalent to 5 percent and the other to 6 percent of the total impounded premiums. However, these two checks to each company had been canceled, and in place thereof one check for the 11 percent finally issued. When this was called to the attention of Folonie, he explained that Street had instructed the bookkeeper to prepare these two checks for each company as described above, for what reason he could not state, however; that when he had discovered this, he had informed Street that since he was responsible as a co-trustee he could see no reason why two checks for each company were necessary; and although Street became very angry at his interference he had the two checks canceled and one sent to each company. This little incident was very interesting, because rumors were current that the payoff had been about 5 percent of the total impounded premiums. It appeared that Street, who by the way had originally requested that no accounting be required of this trust fund, had in mind sending the companies two checks, one of which would be for 5 percent of the total impounded premiums, and possibly to have them return this check, endorsed to him, for the payoff. If these were his plans, they were voided by the action of Folonie.

A list of the 137 fire insurance companies and the amount of impounded premiums of each company had been obtained from the custodian of the fund. If the payoff was 5 percent of the impounded premiums, the total would be approximately $450,000. One of the treasury agents was assigned to visit each of the insurance companies and by an examination of their books determine whether any payments had been made and to whom. The other two treasury agents began a thorough investigation of the financial affairs of Street.

It was readily discernible that the treasury agents would be met by a passive resistance and that every obstacle that could legally be used would be placed in the path of their investigation. Too much was at stake. If a payoff in connection with the compromise of the rate litigation had been made, not only would the fire insurance companies be involved in a scandal but the court might void the settlement with a possibility that they would have to replace the funds in the custody of the court, which would mean returning over $7 million. Word spread around rapidly that an investigation was in progress. Outwardly the agents were treated courteously, and they received what they asked for, but were given no assistance beyond that.

The administrator of the Charles R. Street estate was the trust department of the City National Bank and Trust Company of Chicago. A request was made by the treasury agents for all of the canceled checks, check stub books, and other records of Street. They were informed by the trust officer that no such records had been found after the death of Street, and that he was experiencing difficulty in preparing the current income tax return of Street due to the lack of records. It was therefore necessary to analyze the bank accounts of Street, and a summons was issued on the City National Bank and Trust Company to produce all his personal bank accounts. The ledger sheets containing these bank accounts were kept in bound volumes, alphabetically arranged, and the volumes containing the ledger accounts of Street were produced. A transcript was made of them. While transcribing his bank accounts for the year 1936, one of the treasury agents discovered that immediately following the last ledger sheet of that bank account, another account under the name of Charles R. Street Agency followed. The bank official in whose custody the record was kept while the transcription was being made immediately informed the treasury agent that the summons covered only the personal bank accounts of Street and that he could not allow him to examine this agency account, which was not considered a personal account. However, the treasury agent had seen enough of the ledger sheet to notice that this agency account, although ordinarily having a daily balance averaging about $60, suddenly during one week in March 1936 had daily balances in excess of $100,000.

A new summons was issued on the bank requesting the production of the Charles R. Street Agency account. A conference was held with the attorneys of the bank, and the treasury agents were informed that a decision would be reached that afternoon whether or not the desired records would be produced. When the appointed time came, the bank officials informed the treasury agents that they had been in contact with the officers of the Great American Insurance Company to whom this agency account belonged, and that the officials of that insurance company had suggested that the agents call on them. Accordingly, the following day the agents visited the offices of the Great American Insurance Company and, after stating their desire to see the books and records of that company, were informed that all the records would be made available to them. An examination of the cash receipts and cash disbursements journals of the company did not disclose any deposits or withdrawals of amounts such as was disclosed by the agency bank account. The general ledger contained an account captioned "Charles R. Street Agency Account," but the entries posted to this account, with no folio references, did not disclose the posting of any balances in March 1936 reflecting the large amounts disclosed in the agency bank account. After further questioning the bookkeeper finally admitted that a separate receipts and disbursements journal had been kept for any agency account which reflected collections of premiums made by Street personally. At the close of each month a statement of the debits and credits to this account for the month would be prepared and submitted to the general offices of the Great American Insurance Company and any balance on hand would be transferred to the regular accounts of the company. These records were produced.

The agents found that from March 23, 1936, to March 31, 1936, receipts of money were debited in this book as follows:

March 23, 1936	$ 44,916.88
March 24, 1936	115,891.89
March 25, 1936	58,418.24
March 26, 1936	60,530.54
March 27, 1936	18,954.01
March 28, 1936	16,675.06
March 31, 1936	1,671.92
Total	$317,061.54

On each of these dates a similar credit entry appeared, revealing that the money was deposited and withdrawn the same day. In order that the total debit and credit postings to the general ledger and that the monthly report to the company would not disclose such large amounts debited and credited, the withdrawals of these funds, instead of being credited to the account, were placed on the debit side in red ink. This manner of making entries would result in the debits and credits reflecting only the usual entries, the large and unusual debits being offset by the red figures. The situation now became tense, for the agents realized they had discovered a fund of $317,061.54 which, by the manner in which the entries were made, disclosed an attempt at concealment.

The bookkeeper was requested to produce the checks covering the disbursements of this money. He explained that those checks had been filed separately from the regular checks and that he would have to go to the basement to obtain them. He appeared nervous and before leaving inquired whether it was absolutely necessary that the agents see those checks. He was gone a considerable time and when he returned he was accompanied by G. D. Gregory, secretary of the Great American Insurance Company. Gregory informed the agents that he knew they had a perfect legal right to see those checks, and that it was not his desire to keep the agents from seeing them; however, out of respect to the late Street he would like to delay the matter and, since he understood that the agents would have to make an accounting to their superior officers for any delay, he suggested that a letter be written to him requesting the production of these checks; that he would then submit this letter to the general counsel of the company located in New York, and that it would be possible in that manner to delay the investigation for a considerable length of time. Gregory was immediately informed by the agents that there was a U.S. statute covering the willful impeding of an investigation, and the agents departed, intending to inform the New York office of the Intelligence Unit to issue a summons immediately upon the home office of the Great American Insurance Company in that city, requesting the immediate production of all the books and records of the branch office in Chicago, and also to discuss the matter with the U.S. attorney.

While the agents were in their office in the Federal Building getting ready to get in contact with the New York office, a telephone call came from Gregory requesting that the agents return to his office immediately. Gregory was informed that this was impossible, that one of the agents had left the office for lunch, and that they could not return to Gregory's office before 1:30 P.M. Gregory seemed to be very insistent that the agents should immediately return to his office, and repeatedly asked whether the agents were or had been in conference with the U.S. district attorney. About 2:00 P.M. the agents returned to the offices of the Great American Insurance Company and there they were given photostatic copies of the checks requested and also photostatic copies of book entries covering these checks. When questioned why Gregory had so suddenly changed his mind about the production of these records, Gregory stated that after the agents had departed he had discussed the remark of the agents about impeding a federal investigation with other officers of the company and they had suggested that the agents be given the records immediately before they could take any action through the U.S. district attorney.

An analysis of the canceled checks produced disclosed that Street cashed these on April 1, 1936, in an aggregate amount of $317,061.54. On the same date he had borrowed $20,000 from the City National Bank and Trust Company which he deposited and had drawn an amount of $12,950.23 from the bank account, and that therefore on April 1, 1936, he had in his possession $330,011.77. It appeared apparent, from the fact that he personally had borrowed money on that date, on which loan he had to pay interest, when ordinarily he was very careful about unnecessary expenditures, that on April 1, 1936, he urgently had needed $330,000. It was later learned that some of the fire insurance companies were slow in remitting their 5 percent allotment, making it necessary for Street to borrow the money. In order for the bank to cash such a large amount of checks, it was necessary for them to obtain additional money from the Federal Reserve Bank in Chicago. From the Federal Reserve Bank it was learned that the bills were all of $100 denominations and the serial numbers of these bills were obtained, but since these bills were $100 Federal Reserve notes it did not appear at that time that this evidence would be of any value.

An analysis of the deposit tickets covering the deposits in the Charles R. Street Agency account for the period March 23 to March 31, 1936, disclosed that the deposits consisted of numerous checks from fire insurance companies. These items were sent to the agent examining the records of the companies to facilitate the search for the payments made by them to Street. Insurance companies usually have numerous separate accounts, for which separate bank accounts are kept, and a knowledge of the date and the amount paid made the task less difficult for the agent assigned to this phase of the investigation. Especially was this true because, due to the passive resistance encountered, no assistance could be expected from the officials of the fire insurance companies.

When this agent had completed his assignment, evidence had been secured by him that in 1935 the fire insurance companies had paid Street $100,500 and that in 1936 they had paid him $347,000.

It was now known that Street had received $447,000 in 1935 and 1936 from the fire insurance companies, all of which he had converted into currency, but there was still no evidence as to what he had done with this sum of money. The administrator of the Street estate was again approached and questioned as to whether there were any records, including canceled checks, or memoranda of the late Street in his possession. The administrator stated that after Street's death his son, Donald M. Street, had come to Chicago and gone through his father's desk, and the administrator believed he had heard somewhere that the son had taken some of his father's records with him. The administrator was informed by the agents that they had to proceed to New York in the next few days and would interview Donald Street to determine whether he had any of his father's records. The following day the agents departed for New York and immediately upon arrival there visited Donald Street at his offices in the Guarantee Trust Company, serving him with a summons to produce all records belonging to his father that were in his possession. Donald Street informed the agents that he was sorry but he had received notice the day before to send these records to Chicago and that his secretary had sent them by express. The secretary was seated in the same room and Street, apparently to confirm his statement, turned to his secretary and asked her whether she had sent the records by express, and to his amazement she replied that they were still in the office since she had not had time to take them down to the express office. There was nothing else for Street to do but to turn the records over to us.

An examination of these records disclosed that they consisted of check stub books for the years 1935 and 1936 and also canceled checks for two months, October and November 1936. A transcript was made of the check stub book and of the canceled checks. There was one interesting check included among those available, namely, a check dated October 24, 1936, issued by C. R. Street on his personal account for $10,000 payable to the City National Bank and Trust Company. The check stub book of Street covering this check disclosed the following notation: "Trans. to St. Paul. Tax land." However, a careful scrutiny of this entry disclosed that the word "Paul" had been written over some other name which was now illegible. It was also disclosed that Street after his experience in 1935 had made many alterations in his check stub book for the year 1936, apparently due to his desire to mislead the agents. Thus, for instance, on April 1, 1936, in reference to check #7215 which was the check for $12,950.23 which Street had cashed on April 1 at the same time when he cashed all of the fire insurance company checks, he had erased something, but had added in writing, "Bal. Shugrue. Loan and taxes."

The agents discovered a Margaret Shugrue residing in Chicago. Upon questioning her, she admitted that she had met Street in 1937 and obtained a loan from him on real estate owned by her, but that she had not borrowed any money from him in 1936. She was positive that the first time she had had any contact with Street was in 1937, and the real estate records confirmed her statements with respect to a loan in that year. It was apparent that in 1937, when he was harassed and desperate in connection with the $100,000 he had received from the fire insurance companies in 1935, he altered all items on his check stub books in such a manner that the items would not attract suspicion in the event of an investigation. He probably believed that when he made the notation mentioning the Shugrue loan in connection with the check for $12,950.23, an inquisitive treasury agent could be satisfied by an explanation that he had had several transactions with Shugrue, substantiated partially by a record of a loan in 1937.

While in New York the agents interviewed the officials of some of the more prominent fire insurance companies. None of them knew anything about this payment, except that it had been paid at the request of Street. It appeared extraordinary that these companies should pay out almost half a million without knowing the reason for the payment, but the officials stuck to their version. It was found that an employee of Paul L. Haid, president of the Insurance Executives Association, New York, personally had delivered to each of the fire insurance companies in New York City a check for

11 percent of the total impounded premiums which the companies were informed was a partial distribution for the 30 percent trust fund held in Chicago, and they were requested at the same time to give a company check for 5 percent of their total impounded premiums to this employee, this check to be payable to C. R. Street personally. When questioned as to why they should issue a check for 5 percent of their impounded premiums to Street when he had just given them 11 percent of the impounded premiums, the officers of the fire insurance companies stated that they could not understand the transaction, but they understood that Street had some additional legal expenses in connection with the settlement of the case. The officials were informed that under the compromise agreement, the 30 percent trust fund had been set aside for such contingency as the payment of legal fees and that, if the trust fund had sufficient remaining funds to make a distribution of 11 percent of the impounded premiums, it would not be necessary for the companies to refund a 5 percent payment to Street personally. The officials stated that, although the transaction appeared out of the ordinary to them, they had no knowledge of why such a procedure was followed, and most of them stated it should be understood that when Street ordered something they always obeyed. It was further disclosed that some of the officials thought this money had been refunded to them, since they received a check for 5 percent of their total impounded premiums in December 1937, and in many instances the companies had credited this payment against their check issued in March 1936. When it was pointed out to them that this 5 percent check received in December 1937 was an additional disbursement of the trust fund to the companies and had no connection at all with the 5 percent check which had been sent to Street personally, they appeared very mystified, but could give no further information.[2]

Paul L. Haid was interviewed. Haid explained that he was president of the Insurance Executives Association, which was an association composed of the executives of the principal fire insurance companies, and had been formed for the purpose of closer cooperation between the fire insurance companies. Haid stated in April 1935, Street had telegraphed him to arrange a meeting with a number of the prominent fire insurance executives. Such a meeting was arranged on May 2, 1935, and Street advised those present that for some time he had been working with the authorities in Missouri toward the arranging of a compromise of the pending legislation and that he needed funds immediately, and because of the difficulty in making a pro rata assessment against all the companies involved in the rate litigation in such a short time, he was just asking the larger companies to raise a fund of $100,000, which was sent to Street. Haid explained that Street had told him he had to hire some political attorney, but that he did not tell the executives to whom the money would be paid. Street at that time informed the executives that the checks should be made payable either to him or to Hicks and Folonie, and that they were to be charged to legal expenses of the Missouri litigation. In March 1936, Haid said he received a telephone call from Street again requesting him to call together certain named executives. This Haid did, and Street a day or two later met with these executives in Haid's office. Some of these executives were the same as had been in a meeting in 1935. Street told the assembled executives that he was advancing to the companies 11 percent of the total impounded premiums from the 30 percent trust fund, but that he had such heavy expenses it would be necessary for the companies to return to him 5 percent of the total impounded premiums less any contribution made to him in 1935. Street explained that this money would be for expenses which could not be paid out of the 30 percent trust, but he did not give any reason. The executives agreed, although some were surprised that such a large sum was needed, approximately $350,000 in addition to the $100,000 advanced by some of the companies in 1935. Street said, however, it was all the money he would need and he later would make a full accounting of the 5 percent fund turned over to him. No such an accounting was made.

Haid explained that, although it might appear strange to some people that these fire insurance companies would be willing to pay $450,000 without any knowledge as to what the money would be used for, it should be remembered that Street had a reputation for honesty, had a way of making people obey him, also that he was known to be very taciturn and would not discuss any matter with anyone until he thought it was necessary. In addition Haid stated the cost of the litigation in Missouri was costing them quite a bit through legal fees and loss of business, and that if they thought Street could settle it for $450,000, they would be perfectly agreeable and would certainly not antagonize Street if he did not desire to tell them to whom he was paying the money. Haid reiterated that Street was a forceful, dominant character, whom very few people would care to antagonize.

Haid's office took care of the 5 percent checks of the fire insurance companies located in New York City. For those fire insurance companies located in other parts of the country, Street either called by telephone or submitted letters to the executives stating that these companies would receive a check for 11 percent of their impounded premiums but were to return payable to him company checks for 5 percent of their total impounded premiums. In one of these letters, addressed to A. F. Powrie, an officer of the Fire Insurance Company of Philadelphia, with offices in Chicago, Street stated, in part, after demanding a check for 5 percent of the impounded premiums, "Which will mean you have paid me five percent of the total amount of premiums you have impounded in Missouri, but that out of the expense funds, a portion to me and Folonie as Trustees, you have been furnished the money to pay it."[3]

After the evidence had been obtained from all of the insurance companies, the agents returned to Chicago. They were anxious to determine why Donald Street had been requested to send the records to Chicago when it was known by the administrator of the estate that the agents were proceeding to New York. Upon arrival they visited the offices of the trust officer of the City National Bank and Trust Company, but he was absent on vacation. Another officer of the trust department of the bank was approached and asked whether he had access to the records of the trust department. He stated he had, and the request was made of him to produce the correspondence file in connection with the Street estate. This was done and, although no correspondence was found with respect to the New York incident, a letter was found dated approximately a year previous which was addressed to Walter H. Eckert and signed by the trust officer of the City National Bank and Trust Company, stating therein that there were enclosed all of the canceled checks for the year 1936 of Charles R. Street, with the exception of the months of October and November. It will be recalled that the canceled checks for the months of October and November were in possession of Donald Street. A request was made to produce everything the bank had in their possession pertaining to Charles R. Street. Several suitcases were produced from the vaults, and upon opening one of them all the canceled checks of Charles R. Street as far back as the year 1928, with the exception of the year 1936, which has been mentioned previously, were found. A transcript was made of all these checks. Walter Eckert, an attorney, was interviewed, and he stated that these checks had been sent to him for analysis by the administrator of the estate since he was the attorney who represented Street prior to his death. He produced the canceled checks, and a transcript was made of them. Only one interesting fact was noted, and that was a canceled check dated April 16, 1936, check #7228, issued by C. R. Street payable to the City National Bank and Trust Company for $20,000. On the check stub book Street had made an erasure, but underneath made the notation, "Payment on note."

A search of the other suitcases, which contained numerous personal letters and other personal effects of Street, disclosed two items that appeared of interest. One of these items was an adding machine tape on which was written in Street's handwriting, "Total paid," and then the following figures were listed:

$$\begin{array}{rr}
 & \$253,415.90 \\
 & 83,740.04 \\
 & 21,890.51 \\
 & 8,580.20 \\
 & \underline{3,086.57} \\
\text{Total} & \$370,715.22
\end{array}$$

This adding machine tape incurred quite a bit of curiosity. The words "Total paid" and the fact that the figures so closely approximated the amounts which Street had received from the insurance companies caused some speculation as to whether these amounts disclosed what had been paid to others. However, it may be stated here that the mystery of this adding machine tape has never been solved.

A note was also found among his effects stating: "Considerable collateral at bank. Walter Eckert, attorney, 135 South La Salle, will know of cause of shortage to be paid." It appears that this notation was made by Street shortly before his death and was to carry information to his attorney if he should die. When Eckert was questioned with respect to any shortage, he replied that he knew of none and that he had been analyzing the 1936 canceled checks of Street in order to determine the shortage referred to by Street.

Later developments disclosed that Street suffered financially with respect to this payoff. He actually collected only $447,500 from the fire insurance companies, but disbursed in connection with the payoff $460,000, and in addition had paid additional income taxes and interest of $49,918.68 when he filed his amended income tax return reporting the $100,000 received in 1935. He had to sell a considerable amount of his securities to pay the $62,418.68 which he had expended in excess of what he had received from the companies. It was this shortage he was referring to in his note to Eckert.

There was also a typewritten letter found among the effects of Street dated May 16, 1935, but not signed. It will be recalled that the meeting between Street and O'Malley to effect a compromise settlement occurred on May 15, 1935. This letter is quoted as follows:

May 16, 1935

Dear Mr. Street:

I have been giving considerable thought to the matter which we were in Kansas City about this week and trust that you will pardon my offering some suggestions.

I understand that the Governor will be in Kansas City on Saturday of this week and I am writing a letter to our friend, giving him some of the details of this arrangement in order that he may be familiar with them when he sees the Governor on Saturday.

Our friend at Jefferson City informed me that the Governor wants to make sure that this matter is going to meet with the approval of our friend and you can readily see the advantage it has been to make the arrangement which we have made. I do not think there was any way in the world to have accomplished the thing we have accomplished without his assistance.

I would like to further suggest that I am not at all sanguine about Folonie's understanding of this matter. He keeps insisting upon an 80-20 basis when my idea is that all expenses of all kinds should be deducted first and that would leave a balance of $6,300,000, which is to be divided, according to my calculations, 33 1/3% to policyholders or $2,100,000, and 66 2/3% to the companies or $4,200,000. While it is true that the 33 1/3% figure is the same as 20% of the total, it nevertheless is better from a psychological and political standpoint to say that the money is divided on a 1/3% and 2/3% basis rather than on an 80% and 20% basis.

It is my experience with attorneys (although I happen to be a piece of one myself) that they do not always understand how to present a practical proposition to the courts; they are always thinking in legal terms and this, I think, is a matter which is a little beyond that.

I was hoping to hear from you today because if it seemed

urgent, I might drop over to Kansas City and see our friend, in
order to make sure that everything is understood.

This letter contains several interesting items, mentioning a friend
in Kansas City, the home of Thomas J. Pendergast, a friend in Jefferson City, possibly R. E. O'Malley, and it identified the writer as
being an attorney, in view of the fact that in one of the letters he
states, "It is my experience with attorneys (although I happen to be
a piece of one myself)." Furthermore, the envelope in which this
letter was contained was postmarked "St. Louis, Missouri," and it
began to appear that there were three other persons in addition to
Street who knew something about the inside plans of the compromise of the insurance rate litigation case, namely, an attorney in St.
Louis, O'Malley in Jefferson City, and Thomas J. Pendergast in
Kansas City; however, this was not conclusive, and still was based
on a mere conclusion.[4]

In the meantime one of the treasury agents had been endeavor-
ing to trace the $20,000 check dated April 16, 1936, and the $10,000
check dated October 24, 1936, which checks Street had drawn
payable to the City National Bank and Trust Company. Although
both of these checks had been made payable to the bank, the bank
records produced did not disclose what had become of this money.
On July 26, 1938, one of the agents began examining copies of
telegrams sent by the bank during the year 1936. There did not appear to be any apparent reason why it should be suspected that
these copies of telegrams might contain any information; however,
the agent made the examination because at that time he had been
left alone in a basement of the bank while the bank employee who
was working with him had some other duty to perform. In the ab-
sence of this employee he did not have access to any other records
and, in order to pass the time, began fingering through these copies
of telegrams. He found a telegram addressed to the First National
Bank in St. Louis dated October 24, 1936, stating that the City National Bank and Trust Company was crediting the account of the
First National Bank in St. Louis with $10,000 and requesting that
the latter bank pay this sum to A. L. McCormack of St. Louis. Street
was named as the one from whom the money was received.

Having discovered this one item and the manner in which it was
sent, the agent began examining the correspondence files of the
bank, there being no copy of a telegram to cover the item of $20,000

on April 16, 1936. In these files was found a letter dated April 16, 1936, addressed to the Mercantile Commerce Bank and Trust Company, St. Louis, for $20,000, advising that the City National Bank and Trust Company was crediting the account of the former bank with $20,000 "in accordance with our instructions to pay this amount in currency to A. L. McCormack, Pierce Building, your city."

So Street had sent $30,000 to McCormack. A link in the chain had been forged and now there appeared a live person who could be questioned. One incident that caused surprise was the manner in which the employee of the bank appeared to be perturbed that the two items had been traced. Several times he asked what the government would do to McCormack.

Meanwhile, a report had been submitted on the Charles R. Street estate, including as income for the year 1936 the $347,582.64 received from the fire insurance companies, resulting in additional tax of $219,473.89. An immediate assessment was made and the administrator of the estate appealed the matter to the U.S. Board of Tax Appeals.

Seven

Investigation of the Income Tax Liability
of A. L. McCormack

A S SOON AS the treasury agents had discovered the two payments aggregating $30,000 sent to A. L. McCormack at St. Louis, they departed for that city to investigate his income tax liability. They proceeded to the offices of the Charles L. Crane Agency and were informed that McCormack was absent from the city on a vacation. This gave the agents an opportunity to examine the books and records of the partnership in order to determine whether the $30,000 received from Street was included in the income of the partnership. It was known from the income tax return of McCormack for the year 1936 that the $30,000 was not reported by him as an individual, unless it was included in his income from the partnership.

Within a few days McCormack, who probably had been informed of the investigation by one of the partners, returned to St. Louis and, when interviewed, stated that on July 27, 1938, he had filed an amended individual income tax return for the year 1936, reporting thereon the $30,000 received from Street and had paid additional income tax of $7,540.82.

This filing of an amended return was very interesting to the treasury agents in view of the fact that the amounts received by McCormack from Street were found in the City National Bank and Trust Company of Chicago on July 26, 1938, and that the amended return was filed the following day. It was discovered that from the period of July 22 to July 26, 1938, McCormack and his family were registered at the Edgewater Beach Hotel in Chicago, and from July 28 to July 30, McCormack alone was a guest at that hotel. Since he personally filed his return on July 27 in St. Louis, he must have returned to St. Louis for that express purpose. It is still a mystery as to

50

the manner in which he obtained the information that the treasury agents had discovered the $30,000 sent to him by Street.

The treasury agents now began a thorough investigation of the finances of McCormack. Since he had been employed at a salary prior to 1925 and since the year 1925 he had been a partner in the Charles L. Crane Agency, it was possible to determine accurately what his total income from known sources amounted to from the year 1919, when he obtained his first regular employment, up to and including the end of 1936. It was also possible, by examining all the brokerage accounts of McCormack, to prepare a complete record of all his investments from the year 1924 up to the close of the year 1936. It was discovered that during the years 1935 and 1936, in fact from May 15, 1935, to September 5, 1936 (in the period when Street had so much currency available), McCormack had used a large amount of currency which did not come either from his partnership account, his bank accounts, or any of his investments. He deposited in his bank accounts during the years 1935 and 1936, $17,420 in currency, deposited in his brokerage accounts $52,560.37 in currency, and paid to a real estate agent for the erection of a home $15,000 in currency, a total of $84,987.37. It was very significant that the first currency used by him was on May 15, 1935, on which date he deposited in his bank account $2,000 in currency. It was also significant that the last currency used by McCormack was on September 5, 1936, at which time he deposited $500 in his bank account. In examining the records of McCormack, it was noted that he ordinarily paid all of his expenses by check and deposited all of his funds received from the partnership account or from his investments in his bank or brokerage accounts. It therefore seems strange that from May 15, 1935, up to and including September 5, 1936, he should have used so much currency which came from an unknown source. It was realized, from remarks made by McCormack, that he would claim that this currency was an accumulation of currency placed in his safe-deposit box in a prior year. For that reason a thorough examination was made of his income and investments in order to be able to disprove that such a large amount of currency could have been placed in his safe-deposit box. The investigation produced such satisfying results that the treasury agents were able to prove, by taking the total income for the years 1919 to 1934, inclusive, and deducting therefrom known expenses and new investments, that he had remaining $53,253.84, or for the sixteen years an average of $3,328.36 per annum. This sum was available for living expenses and some of it could have been placed in a safe-deposit box. However, from 1919 to 1934 he only had $53,253.84 available and, ridiculous as it sounds, if it were conceded that during these sixteen years McCormack, who had inherited no large sums of money, who had a wife and two children to support, and who as an insurance executive had to spend quite a bit of money to keep up appearances, had spent not one cent for food, lodging, or clothing, he could have placed in his safe-deposit box only $53,253.84; yet in 1935 he used $27,487.37 in currency and in 1936, $67,500.

In January 1926, McCormack rented a safe-deposit box at the Mississippi Valley Trust Company. An examination of the entries by McCormack into this box disclosed that he seldom visited this box prior to May 15, 1935. In the year 1926 he visited the box but four times, in 1927 once, in 1928 once, in 1929 once, in 1930 four times, 1931 once, 1932 three times (of which two were on the same date), 1933 once, and 1934 none. He therefore did not visit this box on very many occasions to justify the deposit in it of such an accumulation of currency.

McCormack explained that he placed currency in his safe-deposit box over the period of years to keep his wife, who was extravagant, from knowing how much money he had. He apparently did not remember that he had given his wife a power of attorney in 1926 to enter this box and that on April 13, 1926, she actually did visit the box.

As previously stated, McCormack was divorced from his wife in 1929. Examination of the testimony given at this divorce trial disclosed that McCormack accused his wife of extravagance. Her extravagance was another reason why he could not have placed very much currency in his safe-deposit box.

The testimony at the divorce trial brought out some further interesting facts. For instance, McCormack testified,

> When we got married [in 1920] we lived at her mother's house, because I didn't have any money at that time. We had spent all the money I was making getting around to amusements, dances, theatres, things like that. So we decided to get married and I had about $350 at that time.

He further testified that in 1929, when he purchased the residence at his wife's insistence he borrowed $4,000 from the Industrial Loan Company, St. Louis, to make the down payment and gave a mortgage on the balance, and that in 1928 when he sold that property, he was glad to be able to pay off the loan at the Industrial Loan Company.[1]

Throughout all of his testimony, he speaks about his heavy indebtedness. It was further disclosed that on April 9, 1930, he sent a letter to John S. Leahy, his attorney who had represented him in a divorce trial, in which he states he was pressed for money at the time, and that he did not know where the money would come from to pay for the appeal, which was taken to the circuit court of appeals.

Examination of the assets and liabilities of McCormack which were developed during the investigation disclosed that in those prior years he owed the banks large sums of money, borrowed money from the Industrial Loan Company where he had to pay 8 percent interest, and even borrowed money on one of his insurance policies, a method usually resorted to only in the last extreme. It was during this period that he claimed he had been accumulating currency in his safe-deposit box.

With respect to the $30,000 received from Street, it was disclosed that McCormack would not accept this money from the banks by check.

The $20,000 on April 16, 1936, which was sent by a credit advice from the City National Bank and Trust Company to the Mercantile-Commerce Bank and Trust Company, St. Louis, was paid to McCormack at the latter bank in currency, McCormack signing a receipt.

When the official of this bank was interviewed, he admitted that the procedure was extraordinary, since it was a policy of all banks to make payment in cases like this by cashier's check or bank draft and, if the recipient desired, he could cash this check or draft; however, the bank records would be complete insofar as evidence of payment would be substantiated by endorsement of the check. He admitted that having a taxpayer sign a receipt for currency would entail the keeping of another record, a receipt book. He stated, however, that McCormack had been insistent that this payment be made in currency and refused to accept a check.

The payment of the $10,000 from Street, which was transmitted through the First National Bank and Trust Company of St. Louis, was made in the form of a cashier's check. The official of the First National Bank stated that McCormack had insisted on being paid in currency, but the bank had flatly refused, stating that their custom was to issue a cashier's check and that McCormack would be entitled to cash this check immediately if he so desired, but that a check must be issued. The records of this bank disclosed that on October 24, 1936, they issued cashier's check 798481 for $10,000, which McCormack endorsed and cashed on October 26, 1936.

An interesting development, and one which was later to be of vast importance, was observed with respect to this $10,000. The $20,000 received from Street was converted into currency and was probably included in the deposits of currency made in his brokerage and bank accounts. But with respect to the $10,000, no trace of what McCormack had done with this money could be found. He had ceased using currency in his deposits and expenditures on September 5, 1936. Furthermore, he did not enter his safe-deposit box from September 22, 1936, until December 17, 1936. Thus, he had not placed this currency in his safe-deposit box, nor had he spent it.

McCormack was interviewed several times. On each occasion he was asked from what source these currency expenditures made by him came, but his only reply was that they were an accumulation over a period of years and, when questioned as to whether he had any knowledge of the Missouri rate litigation, he stated that he had been interested only insofar as the fire insurance salesmen were concerned about their commissions and, although he admitted an acquaintanceship with Street, he denied that he had ever handled any currency or money of any description for Street. With respect to the $30,000 received from Street, McCormack stated that he had not reported it because he considered it a gift and that Street had told him he need not report it because he (Street) was not claiming it as a deduction. When questioned as to what services he had rendered in obtaining the $30,000, McCormack stated that he, through his position as president of the Missouri Association of Insurance Agents, had been able to keep the agents from filing suits against the fire insurance companies for collection of commissions due them on the impounded premiums and that Street had paid him this sum for this consideration.

Throughout all of the interviews McCormack was very arrogant and on several occasions demanded to know why the government was making such a thorough investigation of his affairs. On one occasion he made the remark that if he had not feared the possible consequences, he would have been able to have stopped the investigation the night before when the three treasury agents leaving the office had passed directly in front of his automobile. He stated that it only would have been necessary for him to have "stepped on the gas" and the investigation would have ended. Toward the close of one of the interviews he became very furious with respect to questioning him about this $30,000 being received from Street and stated that, although he had filed an amended income tax return reporting this income, he was now preparing a claim for refund since he did not believe that this money was taxable. He stated that he had filed the amended return not because he understood the investigation was in progress but because he had remembered some articles in a magazine about the government investigating Al Capone and that he believed it safer to report this income, thereby avoiding difficulties with the government, although he still insisted that the money was not income to him.

On one of the occasions when McCormack was being interviewed at the Federal Building in St. Louis, one of the treasury agents visited the offices of the Charles L. Crane Agency and, under the pretext that he was required to submit a letter immediately, had the secretary of McCormack write a letter on the typewriter that she used for McCormack's business, forming the letter in such a manner that the words occurring in the unsigned letter found among the effects previously referred to would be contained therein. Comparison between this specimen and the unsigned letter found in Street's effects disclosed that they had been written on the same typewriter. It was therefore apparent that McCormack had had more than a passing interest in the compromise offer and that he was acquainted with "the friend" in Jefferson City and "the friend" in Kansas City alluded to in this letter. Furthermore, McCormack was an attorney, although not practicing as such, and was admitted to the bar.[2]

At this point it appeared advisable to halt the investigation of the income tax liability of McCormack and to submit a report recommending his prosecution for evasion of income taxes for the years 1935 and 1936, based on the currency used by him during these years which did not come from any known source. It was believed that such action might cause McCormack to disclose the source of this money and also to give testimony with respect to the disposition of the balance of the fund in the possession of Street. Such a report was prepared and submitted, disclosing that McCormack owed additional income tax of $7,077.35 for the year 1935 and $19,905.64 for the year 1936 (in addition to the $7,540.82 paid on the amended return). These additional taxes were caused by including as income the currency used during the years 1935 and 1936.

In the meantime it had been discovered that McCormack stayed at the Palmer House in Chicago whenever he visited that city. One of the agents examined the records of that hotel. He found that on January 22, 1935, McCormack had registered at 8:10 A.M., was assigned room 1475-W and departed on January 23, 1935 at 1:42 P.M. On January 22, 1935, he had called Grand 1131 at Kansas City, the telephone number assigned to Pendergast's office at 1908 Main Street. On January 23, 1935, the records disclosed a call from McCormack's room to the Congress Hotel, Chicago, and another call to 1908 Main Street. The Congress Hotel records disclosed that on January 23, 1935, Pendergast and his wife registered there at 9:00 A.M. and were assigned rooms K-1-2 and 4. They departed January 24, 1935.

On March 28, 1935, Pendergast again registered at the Congress Hotel. From his room he had placed a call for the Stevens Hotel, where it was found McCormack had registered the same day.[3] On May 9, 1935, McCormack again was at the Palmer House, arriving at 8:00 A.M., and departing at 3:08 P.M. At 9:04 A.M., April 1, 1936, he again was at the Palmer House, departing at 11:49 A.M. The Pullman Company records disclosed he reserved a seat from Chicago to Kansas City on the "Chief" of the Santa Fe Railroad which left Chicago at 12:01 P.M. and arrived in Kansas City at 9:45 P.M. April 1, 1936, was the date Street had cashed sufficient checks to have in his possession $330,000 in currency.

Another interesting development was that on April 2, 1936, the day following McCormack's trip to Kansas City from Chicago, he entered his safe-deposit box in St. Louis at 9:47 A.M. and two weeks later deposited $31,000 in currency in his brokerage accounts.

It was also revealed that McCormack and Street had registered at the Muehlebach Hotel on May 14, 1935. An interesting event occurred while the records of the Muehlebach Hotel were being examined. The records were kept in a subbasement, below the main basement. There were few lights in this subbasement, in which were stored broken furniture and such other articles not in use. To get to the place where the records were kept, the treasury agents had to proceed down a stairway from the main basement, there being no elevator service below that point, and to pick a devious course among all these objects into a far corner. The auditor of the hotel led the agents to this site where the records were maintained and then withdrew, leaving them as the only occupants of that floor. The agents had just obtained the necessary records preparatory to taking them to the auditor for permission to take them out to have them photostatted, when a terrific explosion occurred, reverberating with an ear-splitting noise in the confined space of the subbasement, and the place was plunged in darkness. In the pitch-darkness the agents groped their way, hoping to find the stairway. They were reluctant to use matches, since the explosion might have been caused by gas. They also were not sure that if they found the stairway they could get out, because on the way down they had noticed the large fire doors which would close in case of fire, and if the explosion had caused a fire, only the auditor knew they were in the subbasement.

With these thoughts in mind the agents groped, stumbled, tearing their clothing against sharp projecting objects, until finally the stairs were reached. Ascending the stairs to the main basement, they saw employees of the hotel using candles to illuminate the place while examining a dynamo which had blown out, causing all the lights in the hotel to be extinguished. The agents breathed a sigh of relief as they left the hotel to have photostats made of the records.[4]

Eight

Investigation of the Income Tax Liability of Thomas J. Pendergast

ORE AND MORE it became apparent that Pendergast was connected in some manner with the payoff in the fire insurance rate case. Street had said he could not say anything about the disposition of the $100,000 until the *Queen Mary* docked, on which Pendergast had been a passenger. Street had also intimated that the money had gone to a Missouri politician. McCormack had called Pendergast by telephone from Chicago, and then on the date Street had $330,000 available McCormack had been in Chicago and taken a train from there to Kansas City.

In addition, while in New York in April 1936 preparatory to going to Europe, Pendergast told reporters that he had approved the compromise of the fire insurance rate litigation, intimated that he had virtually ordered O'Malley and Governor Park to accept a compromise, and stated that the compromise was beneficial to the people.

The treasury agents proceeded to Kansas City and opened an investigation of the income tax liability of Pendergast. One of the first noteworthy things that was discovered was that Pendergast transacted all of his business in currency and that in 1934 he was indebted to banks and individuals in excess of $500,000. In 1935 and 1936 most of these loans were liquidated, all being paid in currency. It was also disclosed that other currency expenditures of Pendergast were greatly in excess of the income reported on his income tax returns. Examination of the Western Union Telegraph Company records disclosed that Pendergast daily sent remittances to bookmakers in the East, averaging $2,000, $3,000, and $5,000 a day, and at times as much as $10,000 a day, this money representing bets placed on horses. From all indications Pendergast was losing on these horse races practically every day. Seldom, if ever, was there any money returned from these bookmakers to Pendergast. All payments to the Western Union Telegraph Company for these money orders were made in currency, and this amount alone exceeded the income reported by Pendergast on his income tax returns. In addition to that, there was the liquidation of the loans previously referred to and the other expenditures made by him, namely, during this period he made two trips to Europe, first on June 7, 1935, when he sailed on the steamship *Normandie,* and the second time he left on April 23, leaving England on May 27 on the *Queen Mary,* which was making its maiden voyage, and arriving in New York on June 1, 1936.

After returning from Europe in 1936, he remained in the East to attend the Democratic national convention in Philadelphia. On June 24, 1936, while attending the convention, he became ill and was taken to a hospital in New York City. On September 10, 1936, he was brought to Kansas City on a special train chartered from the Pennsylvania Railroad and, upon arrival in Kansas City, was taken immediately to the Menorah Hospital, where he remained until the latter part of November 1936.[1]

Examination of the records of the Waldorf-Astoria Hotel, where Pendergast stayed while in New York, disclosed that he paid $1,250 per month for rooms. It was also disclosed that he cashed Western Union Telegraph money orders for $15,000 and $20,000 which were wired to him from Kansas City by his secretary, Gnefkow. An interesting item was conveyed that at one time Pendergast, not desiring to have too many people know of his gambling activities, told the Waldorf-Astoria that any calls coming in under the name of Tom Sullivan would be accepted by him. Also, one of the telegraph money orders, at the request of Pendergast, was sent by Gnefkow in the name of Tom Sullivan which money order was endorsed "Tom Sullivan" in the handwriting of Pendergast.

An analysis of all the currency transactions revealed that in 1935 he had received in currency from dividends, loans, and other known sources of income $125,633.79, but that during this year he had paid out in currency $693,243.65; and for the year 1936 he received currency from known sources in the amount of $183,885, whereas for that year he paid out in currency $797,567.14. Thus, in 1935 he had used $567,600.86 and in 1936, $613,682.14 more in currency than he received from known sources.

Betting on horse races had become a mania with Pendergast. Every noon he went into retirement in his inner office at 1908 Main Street and there, closeted with a handicapper named Roy T. Offutt, the racing sheets were scanned, the previous records of the various horses racing that day were analyzed, and then wagers placed at the various racetracks throughout the country. On several occasions his family strenuously objected to this gambling habit of Pendergast, and on those occasions he would solemnly promise to stop, but the following day as the noon hour approached he would become restless and finally, not being able to withstand the temptation any longer, would retire to the inner office with Offutt. There, undisturbed and forgetting the cares of being a leader of a mighty political machine, he would again indulge in the sport of kings, incidentally paying well for this privilege.

His gambling activities were, in fact, commonly known to many. *Collyer's Eye*, a paper devoted to sports published in Chicago, contained an article in the edition of September 14, 1935, as follows:

TOM PENDERGAST BETS
$2,000,000
"OVERBOARD" 600 G's

By a Staff Correspondent
New York, Sept. 13—Tom Pendergast, political boss of Kansas City and one of the biggest plungers on the American turf today, has gone overboard for the startling sum of $600,000 during the last 30 days of racing on New York tracks, it was learned from an authentic source today. Further revelations are that Pendergast, at one time a big winner this year, has paid off every cent of this amount, half of it to bookies in New York City and a like amount to Harry Cohen, his betting commissioner, over the phone.

Allegedly playing the handicap figures of Roy Offutt, Pendergast is said to have had only two winning days during the past month, with the only real winner being King Saxon. The total amount of his wagers will run close to the $2,000,000 mark, it is said. One of the biggest bets dropped by Pendergast was on Inflame the day Jockey J. Mann drew a suspension for pulling the two-year old. The same day Pendergast went for a "gob" on Below Zero.

The investigation now assumed such proportions that four revenue agents, P. R. Balkema, Albert A. Helfand, William M. Ruggaber, and Frank G. Rumreich, were assigned to aid the three treasury agents originally assigned.

For the year 1935, Pendergast had reported a salary of $2,750 received from the Ready Mixed Concrete Company, $9,000 interest on bonds, $5,000 on 100 shares of Ready Mixed Concrete Company stock, and $15,000 on 500 shares of stock of the W. A. Ross Construction Company. For the year 1936 he reported a salary of $30,000 from the Ready Mixed Concrete Company, $15,000 interest on bonds, $18,570 on 100 shares of Ready Mixed Concrete Company stock, $25,000 on 500 shares of W. A. Ross Construction Company stock, and $25,000 on 100 shares of stock in the T. J. Pendergast Wholesale Liquor Company.

There were no dividends reported from other companies in which it was alleged he was interested. It was noted, however, that the principal stockholder was E. L. Schneider, who also was secretary and treasurer of these companies, as a result of which he received a large amount of dividends each year. Schneider, who was a comparatively young man, married, and with one daughter, had been brought from St. Joseph in 1927 by Pendergast as a bookkeeper. He had prospered to some extent under the guidance of Pendergast and, as a consequence, was devoted to the latter. It however was absurd to believe that Schneider could have been financially able to purchase so much stock of the corporations as the records disclosed. Furthermore, he did not possess the wealth he would have had, had he received the annual dividends on these stocks amounting to approximately $100,000 per annum. Then there was Matheus, the former secretary to Pendergast, who was spending the last days of life as a nonpaying guest in Pendergast's hotel, owning according to the records 250 shares of stock of the Ready Mixed Concrete Company and reporting dividends of $18,000 per year on his income tax return.

Attempts to reach Matheus by telephone or even by letter met with no results. The clerk of the Monroe Hotel, acting under instructions, took care that no one could get in touch with Matheus. One of the treasury agents went to the hotel to see Matheus, and, upon inquiring for him from the clerk, was told, "You can't see him, that's all," but he did obtain the room number of Matheus during the time the clerk's back was turned for a moment. Another treasury agent, who was not known to the hotel clerk, was sent the following day to serve a summons on Matheus. Since most of the guests of the Monroe Hotel were shabbily dressed, the agent donned old clothing and a slouch hat. After entering the lobby he sat around for a while, the clerk getting the impression he was just another panhandler, either waiting to obtain free lodging or waiting for one of the guests. The clerk paid little attention to him, and when the opportunity presented itself he walked through the corridor to the backstairs without being noticed and mounting the stairs reached the room of Matheus. After he knocked on the door, the old man, who was dressed in pajamas, opened the door, and the agent served the summons on him.

Matheus, weak and trembling, appeared in answer to the summons and, when questioned about the dividends the records disclosed he was receiving, stated a fantastic tale of how he spent this large sum of money on drink and amusements, but finally admitted that the stock had been given him by Pendergast in 1932 and intimated that if the latter ever desired the stock returned to him, he would gladly return it. There appeared to be no question that this stock actually belonged to Pendergast. It was not deemed advisable at that time to press Matheus too much on the subject, as he was in very poor physical condition, being on the verge of collapse once or twice during the interview. His illusory testimony that Pendergast had given him $250,000 worth of stock and that he, poor and needy as he was, was the recipient of dividends amounting to $18,000 per year, was sufficient to prove that he was only acting as a straw party for Pendergast.

Schneider was summoned to appear in connection with the various corporations of which he was an officer. For two weeks Schneider was interviewed. Every detail on the books of the corporation was entered into, but he consistently maintained that the stocks were owned by the persons in whose names they were held, and that Pendergast did not own any stocks not appearing in his name. Furthermore, he stated that the dividends on these stocks were paid to the holders of records and that these stockholders retained the dividends for their own personal use. However, when the personal income tax liability of Schneider was taken up and evidence began to appear disclosing that Schneider did not have the wealth which should have been his if he had received all of the dividends on these stocks throughout the previous year, Schneider began to claim the privileges of the Fourth and Fifth Amendments, refusing to testify on the ground of self-incrimination.[2] This very act of his made the treasury agents feel that they were on the right track in assuming that the stocks held in the name of Schneider were actually owned by Pendergast.

Then one of the agents discovered an error made by a girl employee in the office of the Kansas City Concrete Pipe Company which began to weaken the testimony of Schneider. In that company the stock, consisting of 125 shares, was all owned according to the records by E. L. Schneider, who owned two certificates, each one for 62 1/2 shares. Each year two dividend checks had been issued payable to Schneider, but for the year 1936 it was disclosed that one of the dividend checks, for $3,125, had been issued, according to the cash disbursement journal, to Thomas J. Pendergast. However, the canceled check covering this payment could not be found. Schneider stated that the check must have been misplaced and that the entry on the books was just an error made by a clerk, although he could not give a satisfactory explanation why the clerk would be thinking of Pendergast when the entry was made.

The Commerce Trust Company, Kansas City, had installed a recordak system, and an examination of this system revealed a picture of the check in question. Here it was unmistakenly recorded that this check for $3,125, representing dividends on 62 1/2 shares of stock, had been made payable to Thomas J. Pendergast, endorsed by him and cashed. When Schneider discovered that this evidence had been found and he was questioned as to why a dividend should be paid to Thomas J. Pendergast, who was not, according to the records, a stockholder in that corporation, he became very agitated. He begged that the agents release him, and began to weep. After he had composed himself he stated that he would decline to give further testimony.

The investigation of the records of the Mid-West Pre Cote Company and the Midwest Paving Company disclosed that most of the stock was held in the names of Edward L. Schneider and William S. Broderick. Pendergast's name did not appear as a stockholder.

William S. Broderick, who operates the Broderick Construction Company of Denver, was interviewed by one of the agents. According to Broderick, when he attempted in 1927 to obtain contracts for paving the streets of Kansas City with asphalt, he was told there that without the consent of Pendergast it would be impossible for him to do any business. He obtained the consent of Pendergast, but only after he had agreed to form the Midwest Paving Company and Mid-West Pre Cote Company and to give Pendergast one-third of the capital stock of the corporations. The certificates for the stocks given to Pendergast were placed at his instructions in the name of Schneider. Although the minutes disclosed that Broderick was to receive a salary of $25,000 per annum from the Midwest Paving Company, he had to agree to refund, or kickback, two-thirds of this amount to Schneider for the benefit of Pendergast. At the close of each year Schneider would instruct Broderick to report on his income tax return the $25,000 set up on the books as salary, although he had retained only one-third of this amount. This testimony further weakened that of Schneider. He had testified, with respect to the Midwest Paving Company and the Mid-West Pre Cote Company, that Pendergast had not owned any shares of stock in this corporation, that the stock he (Schneider) had owned actually belonged to him, and that he had received and retained the dividends.

The investigation progressed, and included the Sanitary Service Company of Kansas City, which was an organization for collecting and disposing of the garbage in that city. Paul Patton, who died in 1936, had been the dominant figure in two prior companies which had collected and disposed of the garbage. This contract for the collection and disposition of the garbage expired in March 1936, and Patton could not obtain a new contract without the consent of Pendergast. A new company was organized on April 10, 1936, the records disclosing that Lester Jordan, president of the new company, held most of the stock in his name. On April 20, 1936, Jordan's certificate for 1,608 shares was canceled, and three new certificates were issued, one for 1,200, one for 288, and one for 120, all in the name of Jordan. Two days later, on April 22, 1936, the certificate for 1,200 shares was canceled and four new ones were issued as follows:

Mrs. C. E. Pendergast, the wife of Thos. J.	600 shares
Marceline Burnett, child of Thos. J.	200 shares
T. J. Pendergast, Jr., child of Thos. J.	200 shares
Adelaide [Aileen] Pendergast, child of Thos. J.	200 shares

On his income tax return for the year 1936, Jordan reported the sale of these 1,200 shares of stock to Pendergast for $48,000, claiming no cost and paying a tax on the entire sale price. When Jordan was questioned about this sale, his answers were very evasive. He maintained, under oath, that he had delivered the stock certificates to Pendergast on April 22, 1936, although on that date Pendergast was on his way to Europe. He further stated that at the time of sale Pendergast had given him $28,000 in currency and a $20,000 note, that he had placed $28,000 in currency in his safe-deposit box that same day, and that from time to time he had used some of the currency, entering his safe-deposit box each time, until now only $18,000 remained. Jordan was requested to produce the note and allow the treasury agents to verify the amount of money remaining in his safe-deposit box, to which he reluctantly agreed. That afternoon, when he returned to the office, he produced a note dated April 22, 1936, for $20,000 executed by Pendergast, and then accompanied one of the treasury agents to his safe-deposit box where he showed the agents eighteen $1,000 bills. The treasury agent took the serial numbers of these $1,000 bills and, upon examining the records of the Federal Reserve Bank in Kansas City, it was disclosed that the majority of these bills had been printed after the alleged sale on April 22, 1936. Examining the records of the entries in his safe-deposit box rented by Jordan at the Commerce Trust Company at Kansas City, the agent found that he did not enter his box on April 22, 1936, and in fact had only entered it on two occasions since he had rented the box in 1935, namely, once on the day he had rented the box and the other time during the noon period of the day he was being questioned before accompanying the treasury agents to the bank. On the records of the Waldorf-Astoria Hotel in New York it was shown that Pendergast had registered there on April 20, 1936, and remained until April 23, 1936, at which time he boarded the *Ile de France* for a trip to Europe, returning on the *Queen Mary* on June 1, 1936.

At the same time that the garbage contract was under consideration, Pendergast claimed to have sold a farm in Clay County on which he raised his thoroughbreds for horse-racing purposes.[3] This sale was alleged to have been made on April 9, 1936, to Patton for $73,000. On his income tax return Pendergast stated that the farm had cost him $73,000 when he acquired it in 1932. Helen English, who had owned the farm prior to purchase by Pendergast, stated when interviewed that she had sold the farm to Pendergast in 1932 for $42,000. The record discloses that this property was placed in the name of E. H. Matheus and was transferred to the name of

Pendergast in 1935. Pendergast claimed that he had spent at least $30,000 on the farm converting it into a stud farm and, therefore, there was no profit or loss.

Almost immediately after this alleged sale Pendergast obtained a lease on this farm for ten years at a rental of $1,250 per year. Due to the death of Patton, concrete evidence could not be obtained, but it is apparent that in April 1936, when it became necessary for Patton to renew the garbage contract for his company, he not only, through Jordan, gave Pendergast 1,200 shares of stock in a new company, but in addition allegedly purchased a farm from Pendergast for $73,000, which was immediately leased to Pendergast at $1,250 a year for ten years. This farm had cost Pendergast only $42,000 and, from the evidence obtained, it is doubtful if the improvements were in excess of $10,000. Therefore, after the letting of the new garbage contract Pendergast had not only obtained 1,200 shares, or the majority of the stock in the Sanitary Service Company, but he also had obtained a gift of $73,000 from Patton because from all indications there was no actual sale of this farm.

Some interesting testimony was obtained from Gordon H. Hamilton, who was a stockholder in the Centropolis Crusher Company. Hamilton, who was a son-in-law of Ross, had been employed by the Centropolis Crusher Company in 1934 and had purchased 12 1/2 shares of the stock in that corporation for $1,250. His salary was to be $15,000 per annum. According to Hamilton the interests in this corporation were owned one-half by the Pendergast family and one-half by the Ross family, and both families were to share equally in the profits. Since he was considered one of the members of the Ross family and had been hired by his father-in-law at a salary of $15,000 a year, the Pendergast family objected because the Ross family was not only getting one-half of the profits of the corporation but one of the members of their family was also getting a $15,000-a-year salary. In order to avoid trouble between the two families, Schneider suggested to Hamilton that he turn back his check every month. Hamilton states that every month he turned back his check for $1,250, except the last check for each year, out of which he was allowed to keep sufficient to pay his income tax on the $15,000, which Schneider informed him he had to report as income. The money he turned over to Schneider was then equally divided between the stockholders according to the proportion of their stockholdings.

Nine

Admissions by McCormack and
First Indictment of Pendergast

I N FEBRUARY 1939, Federal Judge Albert L. Reeves of
Kansas City instructed a newly impaneled grand jury to investigate the gamblers operating in Kansas City. Judge Reeves
stated that the gambling, which was not molested by the police,
was a menace to decent society and suggested that the grand jury
investigate the income tax returns filed by the gamblers. One of the
chief gamblers was Charles V. Carrollo, the boss of the north side of
Kansas City, successor to Lazia. In order to present such testimony
to the grand jury, U.S. attorney Milligan asked Charles O'B. Berry,
special agent in charge of the Kansas City division of the Intelligence Unit, for cooperation.

Right at this time the administrator of the Charles R. Street estate
filed his brief with the U.S. Board of Tax Appeals, protesting against
the estate being taxed on the receipt of $470,000 from the fire insur-
ance companies, on the grounds that Street had not retained this
money and that he had paid $30,000 to McCormack. This protest
was printed in the newspapers and created quite a flurry of excitement as it became known that the source of a payoff in the rate case
had been found.

Acting on this information, Milligan petitioned the U.S. district
court at Kansas City to order an accounting of the 30 percent trust
fund created by the compromise settlement of the fire insurance
rate litigation. The court ordered such an accounting to be held and
further instructed the grand jury to investigate any possible fraud
in connection with the settlement.

All of the fire insurance company executives and McCormack
were subpoenaed to appear before the grand jury, and the commissioner of internal revenue, Guy T. Helvering, ordered the treasury

agents to cooperate. All the information and evidence obtained with respect to McCormack's finances and activities was submitted to the grand jury. McCormack appeared before the grand jury. It was learned that he was repeating the same story he had told the treasury agents, namely, that he knew nothing about any payoff, that he had never handled any money for Street, and that the currency he had used in 1935 and 1936 had been accumulated by him in the previous year. His story was not consistent with the evidence that the treasury agents had obtained.

The treasury agents also interviewed McCormack again. In attempting to state what he had done with the $10,000 received from Street on October 24, 1936, he stated to the treasury agents under oath that he had lost the money on wagers at the Fairmount Race Track, Collinsville, Illinois. The treasury agents had evidence that this racetrack had closed its season two weeks prior to October 24, 1936. When this information was given to Milligan, he called McCormack and advised him that unless the latter would appear before the grand jury the following day and tell the truth about these transactions, the grand jury would certainly indict him for perjury.

McCormack was now trapped. In desperation he telephoned his attorney in St. Louis, James E. Carroll, who, not knowing the circumstances, told McCormack that he could not see why McCormack feared a perjury indictment because if he told the treasury agents the truth he certainly could not be indicted. Carroll suggested that McCormack, if he still thought he needed an attorney, should get in contact with Forest Hanna, a lawyer in Kansas City. McCormack attempted to contact Hanna but was unable to reach him. McCormack, who was staying at the Muehlebach Hotel in Kansas City, asked another guest in the hotel lobby whether he knew a good attorney in Kansas City. The guest suggested the name of John G. Madden. McCormack visited Madden at his home that night and explained to him that he was a witness before the grand jury and that he needed legal advice. Madden told McCormack that he represented Pendergast, and that he believed McCormack should rather contact Hanna who had been named by the latter at the start of the conversation. Madden contacted Hanna for McCormack and the latter visited Hanna that night at his home. The following day Hanna appeared before the U.S. district attorney and the treasury agents, and requested that the matter be postponed for a few days in order that he could ascertain some of the facts in the case.

In the meantime James E. Carroll from St. Louis, realizing the seriousness of the matter after McCormack had discussed it with Hanna, also came to Kansas City. The officials of the fire insurance companies were also being interviewed again by the treasury agents, and on March 16, 1939, a conference was held with several of the more prominent ones. They were told that, since they were businessmen of high intelligence which was substantiated by the high positions they held, their story appeared ridiculous that they had paid out practically a half million dollars without knowing to whom the money had been paid. It was pointed out to them that no reasonable man would assume that something like that could happen, and that if they told this same story to the grand jury there was little likelihood it would be believed. The insurance officials became quite agitated and one of them said, "We cannot afford to be indicted in a hick town like Kansas City." Later that night conferences were held between McCormack and the officers of the insurance companies and his attorneys, Hanna and Carroll. On the morning of March 17, 1939, McCormack appeared before the U.S. attorney and the treasury agents and stated that he was ready to tell the whole truth. He testified before the grand jury and thereafter before the treasury agents that he had received $440,000 from Street during the years 1935 and 1936, which he had distributed, $315,000 to T. J. Pendergast, $62,500 to R. E. O'Malley, and $62,500 to himself. He further stated he had received an additional $20,000 from Street, so that his actual share was $82,500. McCormack was in very bad physical condition due to worry over the situation, and further interviews were postponed until the following day. He kept muttering to himself and on one occasion made a remark that the best solution would be suicide.

When he was again interviewed, he gave the following detailed statement of the payoff:

> On January 13, 1935, he visited Mr. O'Malley, who was a guest at the Coronado Hotel, St. Louis. Mr. O'Malley told him that if the fire insurance companies were desirous of settling the pending litigation and were willing to pay to have the settlement made, arrangements would be made through Mr. Pendergast. McCormack offered to see Mr. Street on this matter. He went to Chicago on January 15, 1935, did not register at a hotel,

but went direct to Street's office, where he discussed the proposal of O'Malley with the latter. Street told him he would be pleased to meet Pendergast to make the necessary arrangements. McCormack met O'Malley again at the Coronado Hotel on January 18, 1935, and told the latter of Street's desire to meet Pendergast. O'Malley told McCormack he would communicate with Pendergast and suggested that McCormack see Street so that arrangements for a meeting could be made. On January 22, 1935, McCormack went to Chicago; registered at the Palmer House and then visited Street. The latter suggested that a meeting could be held immediately. McCormack called Pendergast long distance at Kansas City from his hotel room, informing the latter of Street's desire for an immediate meeting. Pendergast replied that he would be in Chicago the following day. On January 23, 1935, Pendergast came to Chicago, registered at the Congress Hotel and then came to McCormack's room at the Palmer House, where Street was also a visitor. After McCormack had introduced Street to Pendergast, Street opened up the conversation by giving a lengthy recital of the history of the fire insurance litigation in Missouri and the setbacks and reversals suffered by the fire insurance companies. When he had finished, Pendergast informed Street that he was sure he could convince the proper state officials that the litigation should be settled and Street then asked how much a settlement would cost. Pendergast told Street to make an offer, whereupon the latter offered $200,000. Pendergast refused this offer, but when Street increased the offer to $500,000, he accepted. McCormack took no part in the conversation, although he was present throughout the entire meeting. It was a little after noon, when the meeting came to an end. Before leaving, Pendergast used the telephone in McCormack's room to call his secretary at Kansas City and the latter overheard him telling the secretary to place a bet on some horse race.

On March 28, 1935, McCormack was in Chicago, registered at the Stevens Hotel. While there he met Street. The latter appeared perturbed because the fire insurance rate litigation settlement was not progressing as rapidly as he had hoped and suggested to McCormack that perhaps he had not offered Pendergast sufficient to interest the latter. He told McCormack to communicate with Pendergast and inform him of Street's desire to increase the offer. Later that day McCormack heard that Pendergast was in Chicago, registered at the Congress Hotel. Another meeting was immediately held between Street and Pendergast in McCormack's room at the Stevens Hotel, with Mr. McCormack present. Street informed Pendergast that he was increasing the offer from $500,000 to $750,000, which increase Pendergast agreed to accept.[1]

At the request of Street, McCormack went to Chicago on May 9, 1935, and registered at the Palmer House. Visiting Street, McCormack received from him $50,000 in currency with instructions to deliver the currency to Pendergast and tell him that this represented an advance payment. McCormack took an airplane to Kansas City, met Pendergast at 1908 Main Street and delivered the $50,000 in currency to him. On May 14, 1935, McCormack attended the meeting at the Muehlebach Hotel, where tentative plans for a compromise settlement of the fire insurance rate litigation were drawn up. This agreement was signed and approved on May 18, 1935. On May 21, 1935, again at the request of Street, McCormack went to Chicago, but did not register at any hotel. He went to Street's office, where he obtained another $50,000 in currency from Street with the same instructions as previously received. McCormack took a night train to Kansas City, arriving there on May 22, 1935, went direct to 1908 Main Street where he met Pendergast, to whom he delivered the $50,000 in currency. This time Pendergast retained only $5,000 of the amount given to him, and returned $45,000 in currency to McCormack with instructions to give one-half, or $22,500, to O'Malley and the balance McCormack could retain. After attending the horse races at Riverside Park near Kansas City with Pendergast, McCormack returned to St. Louis.

Up to this time McCormack had not expected to receive any money from Pendergast. The agreement had been between Street and Pendergast that the latter was to receive all the money. All McCormack had expected to receive was approximately $25,000, which Street had promised him for the services he was rendering and of which $20,000 was paid to him by Street on April 16, 1936, as previously explained. Street apparently never learned that McCormack and O'Malley were sharing in the proceeds, which he was sending to Pendergast.

After returning to St. Louis, McCormack met O'Malley at the Coronado Hotel and told him that he had $22,500 in currency with instructions from Pendergast to deliver to O'Malley. The latter appeared surprised as if he had not expected to receive any money in this deal, informed McCormack that he had no place to keep the currency and suggested that McCormack keep it and give it to him in amounts as required. McCormack agreed to do this and after giving O'Malley $2,000 of the currency, placed the balance, $20,500 in his safe-deposit box in an envelope marked as the property of O'Malley. Thereafter O'Malley came to St. Louis on numerous occasions at which times McCormack would visit his box, extract the amount of currency demanded by O'Malley and give it to the latter at the Coronado Hotel. In this manner the full amount of $22,500 was paid to O'Malley prior to March 31, 1936. On February 1, 1936, the compromise agreement was approved by the Federal Court at Kansas City.

During the latter portion of March 1936, Street requested that McCormack come to Chicago on April 1, 1936. McCormack did this, registered at the Palmer House and proceeded to Street's office. There Street gave him $330,000 in currency and told him to deliver this sum to Pendergast. He left immediately for Kansas City, arriving there about 9:00 P.M., took a taxicab to 5650 Ward Parkway, Pendergast's residence, and gave the currency to Pendergast. The latter retained $250,000 and gave McCormack $80,000, again instructing him to give one-half, or $40,000 to O'Malley. McCormack returned to St. Louis the following morning, April 2, 1936, and placed the $80,000 in currency in his safe-deposit box, in two envelopes, each one containing $40,000. On April 9, 1936, he received word from O'Malley that the latter would arrive in St. Louis about 3:00 P.M., and drove to the Union Station to greet him on his arrival. Mr. and Mrs. O'Malley did arrive about 3:00 P.M., and after he had greeted them he told O'Malley that he had $40,000 in currency for him from Pendergast in his safe-deposit box. O'Malley replied that he desired to obtain the money immediately, since he was leaving for Kansas City on the night train and was planning to place this money in his niece's name. McCormack immediately drove O'Malley and the latter's wife to the Mississippi Valley Trust Company, entered his box at 3:33 P.M., extracted one of the envelopes containing $40,000 and returned to his automobile. He then drove to the Coronado Hotel, where the O'Malleys registered at 4:05 P.M., and accompanying them to their rooms, he gave the envelope containing the $40,000 in currency to O'Malley.

McCormack again met O'Malley, who was registered at the Coronado Hotel on October 10, 1936. At this meeting O'Malley informed him that Pendergast was very ill, was a patient at the Menorah Hospital in Kansas City, and had incurred large doctor and hospital bills. O'Malley said Pendergast was in need of money and suggested that McCormack see Street with respect to an additional payment of at least $10,000.[2] McCormack went to Chicago on October 21, 1936, registered at the Palmer House and then, visiting Street, told the latter what O'Malley had said about the illness of Pendergast and his need for money. Street informed McCormack that he would attempt to raise $10,000, but being unable to do so, McCormack returned to St. Louis on October 23, 1936. The next day, October 24, 1936, Street sent McCormack $10,000, which the latter obtained from the First National Bank, St. Louis, in the form of currency as previously described. That night McCormack went to Kansas City, visited Pendergast at the Menorah Hospital on the morning of October 25, 1936, and gave the $10,000 in currency to Pendergast.

McCormack returned to St. Louis. On account of his mental condition, a police guard was assigned to be with him day and night.

The treasury agents continued furnishing more evidence to the grand jury, but it was decided that indictments should be returned immediately against Pendergast and O'Malley charging them with evasion of income taxes for the years 1935 and 1936 by failing to report the money received from McCormack. Accordingly, on Good Friday, April 7, 1939, the indictments were returned.

An earthquake could not have caused more excitement throughout the state of Missouri. The newspapers issued extras, with large-type headlines displaying the fact that the mighty leader of Kansas City had at last been brought to the bar of justice. The *Kansas City Star* had a full-page headline for the first time since the declaration of war on April 6, 1917.

The indictments disclosed that Pendergast had evaded a tax of $185,000 and O'Malley a tax of $7,000. The indictments had a good effect, because with the downfall of the head of the machine, witnesses were somewhat less reluctant to testify.

Frantic efforts had been made to block the indictments. Pendergast's nephew, James M. Pendergast, and Police Director Otto P. Higgins made hurried visits to Washington, but to no avail. The blow had fallen.

Thomas J. Pendergast.
State Historical Society
of Missouri.

1908 Main Street,
the address of
Pendergast's office.
Wedow Collection,
Western Historical
Manuscript Collec-
tion, Kansas City.

Jim Pendergast, standing outside Democratic headquarters at 1908 Main Street. Witmer Collection, Western Historical Manuscript Collection, St. Louis.

Pendergast arranged a new bond issue. *Where These Rocky Bluffs Meet.*

Conrad H. Mann headed the Kansas City Chamber of Commerce. *Where These Rocky Bluffs Meet.*

Henry F. McElroy, Kansas City's first city manager. Under his administration the Ten-Year Plan was launched. *Where These Rocky Bluffs Meet.*

The old courthouse, and the new. *Where These Rocky Bluffs Meet.*

Pendergast's Ready Mixed Concrete Company paved Brush Creek. *Where These Rocky Bluffs Meet.*

Kansas City's Union Station, the site of a June 1933 massacre in which three police officers, a federal officer, and a federal prisoner were killed in broad daylight. *Where These Rocky Bluffs Meet.*

Kansas City's airport, a bonanza for the local concrete manufacturing industry. *Where These Rocky Bluffs Meet.*

The Kansas City Municipal Auditorium, another major project carried out under the direction of City Manager McElroy. *Where These Rocky Bluffs Meet.*

Guy B. Park, governor of Missouri. Photo by Strauss. State Historical Society of Missouri.

Thomas Hart Benton mural, state capitol building, Jefferson City. Benton asked Boss Tom to pose for one of the figures, which Pendergast willingly did. The figure was of a burly man eating dinner. When the mural was unveiled, there was a considerable fuss. Unperturbed, Benton said he had included Pendergast because he was part of Missouri. It looked like the boss was running the state? Well, he was.

"I'VE SELECTED THE NEXT GOVERNOR."

The *St. Louis Post-Dispatch,* like most of Missouri's metropolitan press, was strongly anti–Pendergast, as these cartoons by Daniel R. Fitzpatrick attest. State Historical Society of Missouri, Columbia.

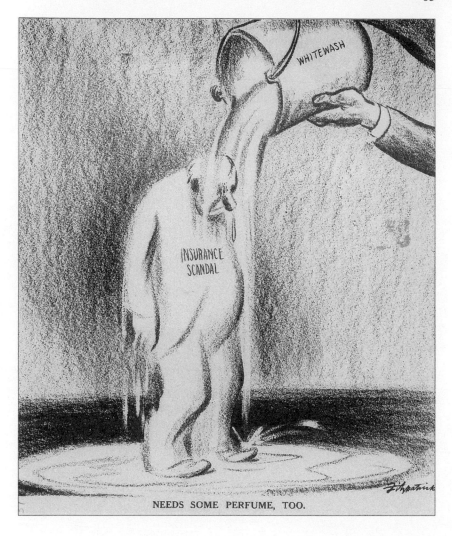

NEEDS SOME PERFUME, TOO.

Maurice M. Milligan.
Kansas City Public Library.

The federal government's investigative team. Left to right: Sam C. Blair, assistant federal attorney; Rudolph H. Hartmann; and Maurice M. Milligan. Wedow Collection, Western Historical Manuscript Collection, Kansas City.

Judge Albert L. Reeves. Reeves papers, Western Historical Manuscript
Collection, Kansas City.

Judge Merrill E. Otis.
*In the Day's Work of a
Federal Judge.*

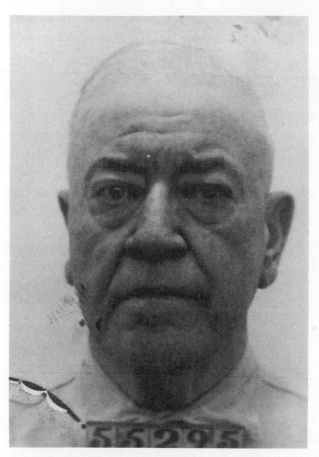

To the horror of Senator Harry Truman, Attorney General Murphy released Pendergast's prison photograph—an unprecedented action. National Archives and Records Administration, Washington, D.C.

Ten

Robert Emmet O'Malley

O'MALLEY, PREVIOUSLY REFERRED TO as the close friend of Pendergast, was born April 12, 1874, at Leavenworth, Kansas. He came to Kansas City at the age of twenty-three and entered the cigar business. In 1925 he disposed of his cigar business and went to Ireland to aid that country in its efforts to free itself from England. During 1926 he returned and entered the general insurance field, in which he remained until appointed by Governor Park in June 1933 as superintendent of the insurance department of the State of Missouri.

During 1901 he married. He had one son, Lambert S., who during 1939 was legal consultant of the Civil Aeronautics Commission with offices at Washington. Prior to this appointment the son had been assistant city counselor at Kansas City.

An investigation of his income tax liability for the years 1935 and 1936 disclosed that he had spent money freely while in Jefferson City, but nothing startling was disclosed until after the admission by McCormack that he had paid O'Malley $62,500 of the payoff money on instructions of Pendergast.

It will be recalled that on April 9, 1936, McCormack stated he had paid O'Malley $40,000 in currency. According to the records, O'Malley registered that day at the Coronado Hotel. Pullman records revealed that O'Malley and his wife left that same night by train, arriving in Kansas City early on the morning of April 10, 1936.

During the investigation, information was obtained that O'Malley had a niece, Adaline A. Cross, residing with her husband, Jess C. Cross, in Kansas City. Investigation brought further information that on April 10, 1936, the date the O'Malleys returned to Kansas

City from St. Louis, Mrs. O'Malley had accompanied Mrs. Cross to the Union National Bank and that on that date Mrs. Cross had rented a safe-deposit box in her name.

Thereafter numerous visits were made to this box by Mrs. Cross, but always accompanied by her aunt, Mrs. O'Malley. During February 1938, Cross, while out riding with the O'Malleys in their automobile, saw a house at 7348 Wayne Avenue, which was for sale. The owner, Carl Schilling, had valued the residence at $18,000, but to make a quick sale was willing to accept $7,500. The property had been placed in the hands of John J. Van Evera, a real estate dealer. Mrs. Cross liked the residence and her aunt, Mrs. O'Malley, offered to loan her money to make the purchase.

They went to the real estate dealer the following day, after first visiting the safe-deposit box, and gave him a down payment of $500, all in $100 bills. The real estate dealer did not notice anything out of the ordinary then, but when Mr. and Mrs. Cross, after Mrs. O'Malley had again visited the safe-deposit box, came to his home the next evening with the balance of $7,000, also in $100 bills, he became suspicious. Having full knowledge of the lawlessness existing in Kansas City, he was afraid that he might be robbed before morning; in fact, he suspected that the entire transaction had been planned. He would sell the property, then be robbed of the purchase price and, as a result, nothing would be left of this transaction. A person had to be cautious in a wide-open city where the police only acted when the boss was willing and where crimes were not investigated when friends of the boss were involved.

He had told Mrs. Cross to bring a cashier's check for the balance of the purchase price and instead she brought seventy $100 bills, crisp and new, still bound together by paper bands on which were stamped the name of the City National Bank and Trust Company, Chicago. The treasury agent listened to this story being unfolded by the real estate dealer.

"Are you positive that these bands had the name of the City National Bank and Trust Company on them?" questioned the agent.

"I certainly am, and here are the bands," replied the real estate dealer.

Yes, he had kept everything, because the transaction appeared so strange to him, currency brought to him under the cover of darkness. The real estate dealer continued with his story. What evidence would he have that this money was his, if he were robbed and later the money would be recovered? A thought struck him. He would take the serial numbers of the seventy $100 bills. So he and Mr. and Mrs. Cross made a record of each serial number.

"Have you the list of these serial numbers you made that night?" he was asked.

"Yes," he replied. He produced the list and these numbers were identical with the serial numbers of the bills Street had obtained from the City National Bank and Trust Company on April 1, 1936.

Mr. and Mrs. Cross were questioned. Certainly they had purchased the property at 7348 Wayne Avenue, and it was a bargain. They had borrowed the money from the O'Malleys, since they had not been able on the salary of Mr. Cross as athletic director at a high school to amass such a large sum of money. Mrs. Cross recalled that the real estate dealer had requested a cashier's check, but when this was suggested later to O'Malley he had told his wife, "No! Cashier's checks can be traced." She also remembered that when the currency had been paid, the "silly" real estate dealer had demanded that she and her husband make a list of the serial numbers, which she later destroyed. Mr. Cross had not destroyed his list, and when he produced it the numbers thereon were the same as those on the list of the real estate dealer.

Mrs. Cross also recalled that on April 10, 1936, Mrs. O'Malley had told her to rent a safe-deposit box in her name, but that Mrs. O'Malley would pay the annual rental. She had never entered this box, but she had often accompanied Mrs. O'Malley to the bank and on several occasions, although she had no desire to pry into her aunt's affairs, she had noticed packages of currency neatly bound together with paper bands.

Lambert O'Malley, with his wife and children, resided in Washington. Of course his mother corresponded with them. After the letters had been read, they were torn up and thrown into waste receptacles, which were later emptied by a maid employed by the family. This maid, out of curiosity, would piece these letters together and read them.[1] Some written during the period March 14, 1939, to April 4, 1939, were so interesting that she brought them to government officials in Washington and later to a newspaper. Although of no evidentiary value, these letters did disclose the frantic efforts being made to halt the action of the grand jury, who were at that time questioning McCormack, and also disclosed what was transpiring behind the scenes. Some parts of these letters refer only to personal matters, which are not relevant to this story, but the following excerpts from them, which were printed in a copyrighted article by the *St. Louis Post-Dispatch* on April 14, 1939, are recited:

Tuesday [March 14, 1939]

My Dearest Ones:
... You can imagine how thick the surmises and gossip is about the G. J. proceedings. You can hear anything, but of course we sift through and through. No one seems to know definitely how far our friend went, but they had things pretty well settled on him and if he did talk he would try to keep us clean. Dad gets almost panicky at times, for they have gone well into yours and his affairs. Don't be uneasy in any way for the big boy is working fine here. Dad enjoys the gossip you get, and especially about the nephew. You can see everyone is looking out for himself. The Agents had O'Neil again yesterday for a sworn statement and he refused until his attorney was present. I am afraid our friend over East should have done the same.[2]

Thursday March 16, 1939

My Dearest Ones:
... He (Dad) gave up going down to the Senator's St. Patrick's Day dinner, for things are pretty tense. The G. J. has been grandstanding the last few days, hoping our good friend will talk. They have made approaches. Jim Carroll is with him here and they are going to tighten the screws. He can't account for $10,000 and they can put him in contempt of court. We heard something at our front door last night at 2 A.M., and there he was. About 4 A.M. he and Dad went for a drive, then separated at 15th and Paseo about 5. They are putting on Mort Jones, Joe McGee, Tony Buford & Lawton to prove Al wasn't so important for the agents.[3] They do not want him but our other friend and hope Al will talk—which he will never do. Dad seems to be considered out of it entirely—thanks to our friend not talking about him at any time. It is generally supposed Dad was sold down the river—T. J. says it is on account of his reputation for honesty.

Did you see anything of Otto Higgins? This thing was probably his mission.

Friday, March 17, 1939

My Dearest Ones:
Dad enjoyed talking with Lambert last night—just to hear his voice. The news you gave was bursting here, and today has

been a terrific strain. We haven't the least idea of the outcome for our friend from the near East is talking and of course we still hope to be kept aloof from entanglements. Dad came out for lunch. I didn't go to the card party, for he seems to be easier here . . . The insurance executives are here still and will do their work this afternoon, intimating the money was voted for use here with one person, and that, I think, is going to be the near East story.

Everything is so guarded I don't know whether you can understand the first part of my letter, and for goodness destroy them, for Dad would be crazy. We will phone you if lightening [sic] strikes in any way. . . . Don't worry, we can weather any gale.

Saturday P.M.
March 18, 1939

My Dearest Ones:

You may get this letter before you get the one I wrote yesterday and I really hope you do, for things were in a very uncertain state then and for the time being, at least, have cleared. Al thought he was sure to be filed on—I hate to use the real word—so Jim Carroll and Forest Hanna as his attorneys were advising a complete story and you can see Dad was between two fires. He has talked very candidly with both his friends—the big one was getting pretty bitter at the other.[4] It came about to a certain extent by the executives of the companies announcing or saying they would tell that the money was supposed to go to one man in Mo. We can't figure out how Al picked up Forest Hanna, but Milligan hasn't promised him everything if Al will tell his story—Dirty rat. The jury adjourned until the 28th of March. As you see Haide will come back.[5] I've never seen Dad go through such anxiety and your letters have been so much to him, as was your call . . . Dad just came in and says no Dis. Atty. can bring an indictment until it has been presented to Washington. I am not sure whether FBI or Atty. Genl.

Monday, March 20, 1939

Got Lambert's two letters Friday and Saturday this morning and was so glad to get more detail about Jerry's visit. John Cosgrove came to the office this A.M. and told Dad one of the assistant United States District Attorneys was out Saturday night and Francis Roach heard him say Dad and you spent more than you were making. Whom would that be or whom would you suspect. Rumors are just thick. Dad just came home at 3 P.M. and told me this.

We haven't found the detail of Al's story to the jury and

thought best not to contact him. The rumor still persists he talked about T. J. No doubt Milligan is in Washington. Truman will fly back Thursday and try to use some influence.[6] It is bad to say the least. Do not refer definitely to anything I write and destroy my letters for Dad is very anxious about this and our phone also. That is the reason we cannot talk to you long distance. Don't worry—as Lincoln used to say, "This, too will pass."

Friday, March 24, 1939

T. J. sent Tom Graves down to St. Louis to have "Boots" Brennan go to Carroll to find out Al's testimony. They would not talk but Brennan met T. J. at the race track this A.M. and Carroll reports both T. J. and Al will be in trouble—Dad seems entirely clear—T. J. is pretty nearly exhausted from worry. Now don't refer to this in any way. Jimmy is flying to see our big friend in Wash tonight.[7] Truman's publicity has been a Godsend to them for the time being anyway and of course Stark's blast about the police surprised everyone, even the reporters had no idea of what he was going to talk about. . . . Do not worry about things here, they will come out all right for us at least!

Saturday, March 25, 1939

I wrote so late last night there hasn't been time for much of interest to transpire . . . As you will see McKittrick has been subpoenaed for Tuesday and of course Al and the insurance co. executives.[8] It is amazing how neutral Dad can remain with his two friends and really it is right for it was the only thing to be done under the circumstances. You can bet as soon as Dad feels he is safe to leave we will be on the highway for he is anxious to get to you folks and talk it all out. He talks to me almost constantly as we drive.

Did Jo O'Brien ever get to Washington? Later—that telephone call may have cost a lot but it was worth every cent of it and more too. Everything seems more complete when we have talked with you about it. Strange about Barnett but Dad feels that way and was glad you thought there was no hurry about it.[9] Word to Graves to 1908 [Main Street, Pendergast's office] is that our 2 friends will be asked to defend themselves. No mention of us yet. Gov. Park is trying to keep away the scare by wanting to make Barker prominent.[10] He gave an interview to the *Star-Times* (St.L.) to that effect.

Isn't this air mail marvelous. It cuts the distance so much if anything could. Physically we are both just Al and not disturbed too much.[11] Just restless and uncertainty and time. When we can hit the highway will forget it.

Our Arizona tourist will probably be home Sunday or Monday night. Every one else is leaving out there so he wants to too. Keep as close to Truman as you can and of course every one here is tickled to death with the situation he made for himself there. It helps a whole lot in the present set-up.

Thursday, March 30, 1939

Dad feels a little less restless today as something may break out anew tomorrow. He knows some very serious work must be done there and apparently is getting off to a good start. Imagine he is hard to talk to, but he could give you a good picture of everything here.

Dad is considering a lawyer, leans toward Hogsett or Paul Barnett. Of course we both prefer J. A., but under the circumstances it could hardly be.[12]

Tuesday, April 4, 1939

My Dearest Ones:

I thought for a moment Dad was going to plan on starting for Washington today. It is beautiful weather and he does feel the need of talking with Lambert. They have not found out what Al's story was. Brewster is working on Hanna for T. J. and John Madden.[13] John phoned 12:10 last night and came out and talked to Dad until about 2. They suggested Dad send his attorney to Hanna. In fact Hanna said he would talk to that attorney and no one else. Dad has about decided to go to Hogsett but had no intention of sending him to Hanna. Brewster will represent T. J. when the time comes—if it does. We are believing Al in no way mentioned Dad and I am guarding him from getting in too deep with the others. It looks now like it might be Al's word against the other man. No one can fathom how he got Hanna. A messenger went to S. L. last night to find out something. I know it is hard for you to not mention all this detail but Dad scolds me for writing—however—has me reading your letters over to him.

Will write more later maybe as developments come along. We enjoy your letters and don't worry for it is bound to come out later OK. John Madden told Dad the D. A. did have to submit for approval in matters of this type.

Lambert O'Malley had the maid arrested for larceny. She was later acquitted when evidence was brought out in court that the letters had been abandoned.[14]

Eleven

Indictment of Jordan, Admissions by Schneider and Matheus, and Amended Indictment of Pendergast

T HE TESTIMONY GIVEN by Lester Jordan with respect to the alleged sale of stock of the Sanitary Service Company by him to Pendergast, and the testimony of Schneider with respect to the stock ownership in the various corporations with which he was connected, were presented to the U.S. attorney. Both were called before the grand jury. Schneider appeared each day before the grand jury for a week after the treasury agents had presented the evidence which was at variance with his statements. Then on Thursday, April 27, 1939, the grand jury heard Jordan and examined the evidence gathered by the treasury agents. As a result an indictment charging Jordan with perjury was returned. There was more turmoil in Kansas City. The question on the lips of the citizens of that city was, "Who will be next?" One can imagine how Schneider felt. He knew that his testimony was also perjured, and the fact that Jordan had been indicted showed that the grand jury meant to get the true facts.

On the following morning Schneider, who was scheduled to appear again before the grand jury, came with his attorney to the office of Milligan and stated that if he could get the permission of Pendergast he would be willing to tell the truth about the financial affairs of the corporations. That afternoon Pendergast gave Schneider permission to testify with the remark, "Protect yourself; enough have suffered already." Schneider then told the grand jury that the stocks of the corporations, with which he was associated, which were carried in his name, actually belonged to Pendergast; that he had reported the dividends on these stocks on his income tax returns, but that these dividends belonged and were paid by him to Pendergast; that the officers of the corporations, including himself, had paid a portion of their annual salaries to Pendergast, although they had reported them as income; and that the sales of the corporations had been understated each year, and not placed on the books, in order that the proceeds of these sales could be paid to Pendergast without the books of the corporations disclosing these payments. With respect to the latter assertion concerning the understatement of sales, Schneider declared that he could not at that time give accurate information as to amount of gross sales understated each year, but that he would examine the records of the corporations and furnish this information on Monday, May 1, 1939, promising to be in the office of the Intelligence Unit at Thirteenth and Oak Streets at 9:00 A.M. on that day.

Schneider, whose continued appearance before the agents and the grand jury caused him to appear haggard and extremely nervous, relaxed completely after he had made these admissions. He jokingly asked the agents how he could possibly correct all these items on the books of the corporations, without messing the records up so that no one could readily understand what had occurred.

On the same day Jordan and Matheus also appeared. Jordan was granted permission to purge himself of the perjury charge, and he stated that the stock of the Sanitary Service Company, allegedly sold by him to Pendergast, had actually been given to Pendergast, without remuneration, for granting the corporation the city garbage contract. Immediately after giving his testimony and returning home, he was stricken by a heart attack, being taken to a hospital. The perjury indictment was dismissed.

Later, after recovering sufficiently to leave the hospital, Jordan explained that on the day the agents had questioned him about the alleged sale to Pendergast and had demanded him to produce the note and the balance of currency remaining from the transaction, during the noon hour he had conferred with Pendergast. He told Pendergast about the fix he was in and the former gave him a note dated back to the date of the alleged sale. When he told Pendergast he also needed $18,000 in currency to show the agents, Pendergast angrily told him he had no money and that he should see Carrollo. Jordan stated Carrollo gave him eighteen $1,000 bills, which he placed in his safe-deposit box and later showed to the agents. On the evening of the day he was indicted, when it was learned that the agents had obtained the serial numbers of the bills, Jordan stated that Carrollo had come to his house and demanded the

$18,000 immediately. When he explained that this money was in his safe-deposit box and that he could not possibly get it until the next day, Carrollo threatened to "take him for a ride." Although Carrollo finally agreed to wait and although the money was repaid the following day, the shock to Jordan caused by the threat had been so great as to effect the heart attack he had suffered. Jordan never recovered from this illness and on December 15, 1939, he died at the age of fifty years.

Matheus admitted that Pendergast actually was the owner of the stock of the Ready Mixed Concrete Company carried in the name of Matheus and that the dividends paid on this stock had been given to Pendergast. He stated that each year an income tax return was prepared for him by Schneider, which he signed, but that the tax was not paid by him since he had no funds. Schneider in his testimony admitted that the taxes on all the returns filed by persons reporting some of Pendergast's income had been paid by the latter.

On April 29, 1939, an amended indictment was returned against Pendergast again charging evasion of income taxes for the years 1935 and 1936, but adding to the former indictment the income received on dividends of stocks held in the names of others. This indictment charged that he evaded income taxes for the two years aggregating $265,465.15.[1]

It was impossible to charge Pendergast with all of the income it was apparent he had received in those years, because the amended indictment had to be returned before the date of arraignment set for May 1, 1939.

Twelve

Arraignment, Tragedy, and Pleas of Guilty

ON MAY 1, 1939, Pendergast and O'Malley appeared before Federal Judge Merrill E. Otis to be arraigned. Both pleaded not guilty. The courtroom was packed with spectators. The court set the Pendergast case for trial June 12, O'Malley's for June 19, 1939.

Meanwhile the treasury agents awaited the visit of Schneider, who had promised to come to their office with additional information gathered from the records of the corporations. Their wait was in vain.

At the moment that Pendergast, his beloved friend and benefactor, stood before the bar of justice pleading not guilty to the charges against him, Schneider was disappearing over the side of the Fairfax Bridge into the Missouri River at Kansas City. His car was found abandoned on the bridge, and on the seat of the car was a bundle containing the records he had promised to bring to the agents that morning. Lying beneath the bundles were two farewell letters, both dated April 27, 1939, one addressed to "Dearest Ann" (his wife) and one to "Dear Phil" (Phil Abry, a close friend). These notes read as follows:

Apr. 27, 1939

Dear Phil

I sure appreciate your & Eleanore's effort to make things easier for Ann and I these last few weeks.

I cant see my way out of it and I think this will be easier than trying to go through a mess that will last through the rest of my life.

Take care of Ann and Helen and help them bear through the

mess. I feel it will be easier for all and they probably will have everything to live on.

See that Ann has a good attorney if she asks you to help her pick one.

May the rest of your days be happy & prosperous.

As ever
(Signed) Ed

P.S. Personal and dont give to any one.
Left note for Ann

Apr. 27, 1939

Dearest Ann

I am sorry but I prey [sic] God will help you and Helen to bear through it all.

This ordeal for the past month is just too much and it is getting worse all the time. I still say I done what I thought was doing no harm to anyone.

I love Helen and you too much to have you go through what might happen to me so please feel that I am resting.

Be brave and bear through this for Helen's sake and I prey that both of you will get along alright.

Lots of love to
Helen and you
Good by
(Signed) Daddy.

The notes were dated the day Jordan was indicted for perjury and when Schneider realized the predicament he was in personally.

An immediate investigation was made of this tragedy. It was learned that on Friday evening, after he had made his admissions (with the consent of Pendergast), he arrived home in a jovial mood, the first time he had been in a happy state of mind since the investigation of the Pendergast case had begun. Thursday night he had been greatly worried, possibly due to the indictment of Jordan, but now all that worry was past. He arrived home on Saturday afternoon greatly agitated. Efforts of his family to cheer him failed and it was necessary to call a doctor, who prescribed a sedative.

On Sunday he remained in the same morose mood, spending most of the day in analyzing records which, he told his wife, the treasury agents wanted. It seemed that he was afraid of approaching automobiles, as if he expected some disaster. When a car stopped in front of his home that Sunday afternoon, he ran from the window and was very agitated until he was told a neighbor had parked his car there. That evening he and his wife went to a steak-fry, where he temporarily obtained some relief from the thing that was worrying him.

When he and his wife returned home from the steak-fry, he took a sedative and retired. He arose early Monday morning, dressed, and ate his breakfast. His wife, who was not feeling well, remained in bed. As he was ready to leave he came upstairs, kissed his wife, from the dresser took a bundle containing the records he had analyzed the previous day, and told his wife, "If you want to call me today, I won't be at the office; I expect to be at the revenue office all day, but I will call you at noon."

Just as he was preparing to leave the home, the telephone rang, which he answered. His wife heard him say, "I am in a hurry; got to be at revenue office at nine; all right, if you have to see me, I will wait here for fifteen minutes."

About fifteen minutes later she heard a car drive up in front of the house, and looking out of the window, saw her husband talking with Otto Higgins, director of police. A few moments later her husband came back upstairs and, without speaking to her, went to a closet and either took something out of a coat hanging there or put something in it. He then left, and she heard two cars departing.

Higgins, when questioned, at first refused to talk, but later stated he had read in the papers of the predicament Schneider was in and had visited him that morning to see if there was anything he could do for him. He stated that Schneider gave no indication that he planned suicide.

To get to the Fairfax Bridge, Schneider had to pass within a few blocks of the Intelligence Unit office.

Two days later a hat belonging to Schneider was found floating on the surface of the river, three miles below the Fairfax Bridge. On May 5, 1939, his body was found washed ashore about two miles below the bridge. There were no marks of violence on his body. He was forty-six years of age on April 27, 1939, which is also the date of the suicide notes. He had one child, a daughter, who was attending school in the East.

On May 22, 1939, chiefly to avoid further investigation by the treasury agents, Pendergast appeared before Judge Otis and entered a plea of guilty to both counts in the amended indictment, the first one being dismissed. He was represented by John G. Madden and R. R. Brewster, prominent attorneys of Kansas City. Judge Otis sentenced him to serve one year and three months in Leavenworth Penitentiary, this sentence to be served, to pay a fine of $10,000, and to serve three years on the second count, but suspended the prison sentence on the second count, placing him on probation for five years, the probation to start after his release from prison. So that Pendergast could arrange his affairs, the court allowed a stay of one week.

Kansas City was dumbfounded. The man who had ruled with an iron hand, who made or unmade senators and governors by a nod of the head, had been sentenced to the penitentiary. His downfall raised the curtain, disclosing behind the scenes such an array of corruption and fraud in the civic affairs of Kansas City as to belie imagination. Millions of dollars paid in graft, padded payrolls, corruption in all public offices. The decent people of Kansas City had now an opportunity to exert their rights. Public officials and employees resigned en masse.

On May 27, 1939, O'Malley appeared before Judge Otis and, as his boss had done, pleaded guilty to both counts of the indictment. He was represented by William G. Boatwright, an attorney. Judge Otis sentenced him to serve a year and a day in Leavenworth Penitentiary, to pay a fine of $5,000 on the first count, and to serve two years on the second count, but the prison sentence on the second count was suspended and he was placed on probation for three years, the probation to start after his release from prison. Execution was stayed until May 29, 1939. Thus the investigation begun May 9, 1938, terminated successfully May 27, 1939.

Pendergast and O'Malley together entered Leavenworth Penitentiary on May 29, 1939. Born in Leavenworth, Kansas, O'Malley returned to his birthplace in the twilight of his life. Both served their respective terms and were later released.[1]

The three-judge court, which had originally approved the compromise settlement of the fire insurance rate litigation, then set aside the settlement, ordered the fire insurance companies to repay the $7 million to the former custodian of the impounded premiums, and ordered that the entire sum be refunded to the policyholders, who had previously received 20 percent of the impounded premiums. The fire insurance companies have appealed this decision.[2]

Later Pendergast, O'Malley, and McCormack were cited for contempt of the three-judge court in connection with their conduct before that court in obtaining approval for settlement of the rate litigation, and were found guilty by the court. On June 7, 1941, Pendergast and O'Malley were each sentenced to two years in prison on this contempt charge and McCormack was placed on probation for two years. These sentences have been appealed.[3]

The State of Missouri also indicted Pendergast for giving and O'Malley for accepting a bribe, but these indictments were later dismissed.

Schneider's testimony that some sales of the corporations had not been reported as income, that expenses had been padded, and that salaries of officers had been kicked back and distributed as dividends to the stockholders, all of these items having reduced the net income of the corporations, made it necessary to investigate the income tax liabilities of these corporations. This was done, resulting in the assessment of additional taxes, but no criminal prosecutions were instituted, since the principal, Schneider, who had falsified the books and records, was dead.

Thirteen

Charles V. Carrollo

W HEN PENDERGAST PLEADED GUILTY and admitted he had received a large sum of money to influence the settlement of the fire insurance rate litigation, the citizens of Kansas City were shocked, but as the investigation continued they were to learn more and more of the corruption and chaotic conditions caused by the machine. The curtains behind which the machinations of the political leaders had operated were now being drawn aside and some of the backstage scenery was being exposed to public view. The citizens were indignant and action was demanded, but witnesses were still apprehensive of what might befall them or their families if they gave testimony against the henchmen of Pendergast.

On the north side of Kansas City, Carrollo still held sway and, as in the days of Lazia, his gangs were more than willing to wreak retribution against anyone who dared to question his authority. Carrollo was born August 24, 1902, at Santa Ristino, Italy, and came to the United States on January 24, 1906, entering at New Orleans. Later he came to Kansas City, where he was married November 13, 1923. He has never become an American citizen.

Upon his arrival in Kansas City he joined the infamous Lazia gang and he soon was Lazia's chief lieutenant. He became the protector of the gamblers operating in Kansas City. Each week the collectors for Carrollo would visit the gambling establishments and receive protection tributes. In exchange for this tribute the gamblers could operate without molestation from the police, the police department being under the control of Lazia and Carrollo, who were often referred to as the real chiefs of police of Kansas City. If at rare intervals a gambler felt he needed no protection and did not pay

105

the required tribute, not only would the police harass him but the henchmen of Carrollo would make life very unpleasant for him. Some recalcitrants just disappeared, never to be heard from again.

Two large gambling establishments had for several years done a flourishing business, namely, the Fortune Skill Ball Salon and Musser & Company. The latter company operated a large number of slot machines. These enterprises made too much money to be subject to only a tribute, so Carrollo convinced the owners of these enterprises that it would be advantageous to them to leave Kansas City and turn over their interests to him and his cohorts. What pressure was brought upon the original owners to surrender their lucrative interests is not known, but Carrollo had his ways and means of using the proper pressure necessary.

He also was a major stockholder in the Glendale Beverage Company, which manufactured soda water, and the Glendale Sales Agency, which is an agency for a well-known brand of beer. Both of these enterprises flourished under the rule of Carrollo, since no merchants dispensing such articles could successfully refuse to use these products exclusively without damage to their property or injury to themselves or their families.

In addition to these ventures Carrollo was active in many other endeavors such as robberies, bootlegging, and even murders.

On March 6, 1935, a foreman of a federal grand jury stated that testimony before that body indicated that Carrollo had sent men to Kansas to kill Michael Lacapra, who was slain because he had testified that Charles Gargotta, Tony Gizzo, Dominick Binaggio, and Tony Lococo, associates of Carrollo, had provided "Pretty Boy" Floyd and Adam Richetti with safe convoy from Kansas City after the Union Station massacre.

On July 11, 1934, Carrollo drove the automobile in which Lazia and his wife were returning to their home and from which Lazia stepped to be met with a hail of machine-gun bullets causing his death. Thereafter Carrollo alone was "king of the north side."

Before 1938 three attempts had been made by special agents of the Intelligence Unit to obtain evidence as to the income of Carrollo. Each attempt ended in failure to gather competent evidence, chiefly because no witnesses could be found who would testify. Fearful of retribution, these witnesses would deny ever having paid any money to Carrollo.

Then in 1936 special agent W. Harold Lane was assigned to investigate the income tax liability of Carrollo. He had filed returns disclosing the net income received by him from the two gambling establishments he was interested in, but he did not report the protection money he was collecting from gamblers. Prior to this investigation special agent Lane had befriended an Italian youth, who formerly had been employed by Carrollo as a collector of protection money.

Pursuant to an oral request Carrollo voluntarily appeared at the office of the Intelligence Unit, Kansas City, accompanied by his attorney, and gave a sworn statement in response to questions, which was transcribed by a stenographer. The questions asked by special agent Lane and the answers made by Carrollo which were material are as follows:

Q. Do you solemnly swear that the answers you will make to the questions about to be propounded to you will be the truth, the whole truth and nothing but the truth, so help you God?
A. Yes.
Q. You may refuse to answer any questions asked you as provided for in the Constitution and any information you give may be used against you in any future proceedings criminal or otherwise, by the Government; is that understood?
A. Yes.
Q. Have you during 1937 and 1938 acted as an agent for anyone whereby you collected money to be turned over to another person?
A. No, sir.
Q. Newspapers have carried inferences that you collected lug or protection money from gambling establishments in Kansas City. Have you collected money from such establishments or have others collected such money for you?
A. No, sir.
Q. Have you collected money from gambling places, or have others collected such money for you which you later paid to other persons or institutions?
A. No.

This information was furnished to the U.S. attorney, Milligan, who presented it to the federal grand jury. An indictment was returned on June 8, 1939, charging Carrollo with perjury. He was arrested by the U.S. marshal on June 10, 1939, and released on $5,000 bond.

In the meantime special agent Lane and his associates kept on investigating the income tax liability of Carrollo. Witnesses were now less reluctant to talk. Slowly but methodically the treasury agents gathered together the evidence to substantiate the receipt of money by Carrollo which had not been reported.

Gambler after gambler was interviewed and their records were examined. Testimony and records disclosed the tribute paid to Carrollo for protection. Rocco Binaggia, who operated the slot machine enterprise, said that one-third of the gross income from slot machines was paid for protection. Even two brothers of Carrollo, Sam and Frank, admitted that they collected money from gambling establishments for Charles Carrollo.

Evidence was obtained which disclosed that during the year 1934 two gamblers opened and operated the Fortune Skill Ball Salon, a gambling establishment which catered to the better class of citizens. This venture was very lucrative. Carrollo made these operators give him a half interest in the business with the added provisions that Carrollo need not make any investment and that he would not be held accountable for any losses if in any year the business should prove unsuccessful. In 1937, Carrollo received over $64,000 as his share of the profits.

To hide this source of income Carrollo ordered that the checks paying this money to him be made payable to others, some being made payable to his brother Frank. The endorsements on these checks bore the name of Frank Carrollo, but they were not in his handwriting. Neither were the endorsements made in the handwriting of Charles Carrollo, but the checks had been cashed at the Merchants Bank. After prolonged questioning of the bank teller who had cashed these checks, it was finally developed that Charles Carrollo had presented these checks without endorsement to him, that the vice-president of the bank had authorized the teller to cash the checks for Charles Carrollo and that later the vice-president had endorsed the checks with the name of Frank Carrollo. The vice-president admitted that he had endorsed the checks in this fashion, leaving the impression that he did this through fear of antagonizing Charles Carrollo.

The operator of the Cowboy Inn, also a gambling establishment, stated that while he was ill in a hospital several men including Charles Carrollo visited his place of business and took over the operation of the gambling devices. The following day his employees informed him that he owed $12,000 to Charles Gargotta, one of the men who had accompanied Carrollo. He had his wife go to the Interstate National Bank and sell sufficient government bonds to purchase a cashier's check payable to him. He then endorsed this cashier's check and gave it to an unidentified man who visited him at the hospital in exchange for the I.O.U. the man presented. The employees of the Cowboy Inn corroborated his story.

Examination of the cashier's check disclosed that it was made payable to W. E. Hutchins, the operator of the Cowboy Inn, endorsed by him and a "John Smith." The last endorsement was in the handwriting of Charles Carrollo and the check had been cashed at the Merchants Bank. The teller who cashed this check admitted that Charles Carrollo had appeared with the check, had endorsed it with "John Smith," and after the vice-president of the bank had approved the endorsement he had given Charles Carrollo the currency. Apparently Carrollo did as he pleased at the Merchants Bank.

The treasury agents finally were able to complete a fair picture of the income Carrollo had received which had not been reported. Their computation revealed that Carrollo had received the following unreported sums of money, chiefly from tribute exacted from gamblers:

Year	Unreported Income	Income Tax Due
1935	$ 70,765.92	$ 22,589.54
1936	95,176.44	55,375.49
1937	96,335.47	52,966.34
1938	199,730.11	115,727.71
Total	$462,007.94	$246,659.08

On July 21, 1939, the federal grand jury indicted Carrollo on four counts for evasion of income taxes for the years 1935 to 1938, inclusive. He was also indicted for violation of the postal laws, based on evidence gathered by post office inspectors. When arraigned, Carrollo pleaded not guilty to the three indictments for perjury, income tax, and postal violations.

On October 17, 1939, the perjury case went to trial. For a day and a half one witness after another testified how they had been forced to pay tribute to the defendant. The witnesses were no longer afraid, because the power of Carrollo was waning rapidly. Carrollo took the stand. He admitted the receipt of money from gamblers, but stated he had not kept any of it since he had to give it all to Pendergast. He also admitted that he had received more money from the gamblers in one year than the treasury agents had charged him with for the four years, claiming that his annual collections were well over $500,000. By these admissions he convicted himself of the perjury charge.

After two days of trial the case was given to the jury. In twenty-five minutes the jury returned with a verdict of guilty. Sentence was deferred until October 20, 1939.

The following day Carrollo changed his pleas of not guilty on two counts of the income tax evasion (two counts being nolle prossed) and postal violation charges to guilty.[1] On October 20, 1939, he appeared before Judge Otis. In passing sentence on the perjury charge the judge said:

> First I impose sentence in case No. 14,578 in which Mr. Carrollo was tried and found guilty by a jury. The indictment in the case charged the defendant with the crime of perjury. The proof of his guilt was overwhelming. Indeed his guilt scarcely was denied, although the defendant put the government to the great expense and labor involved in a criminal trial. No one was surprised that the jury almost immediately after the submission of the case returned its verdict of guilty.
>
> The maximum punishment which the law provides for this crime is five years' imprisonment and a fine of $2,000.
>
> There are some crimes which are properly regarded by every citizen as in their very nature serious and gravely threatening to the well-being of the state and organized society. Perjury always has been so regarded. It has been condemned by the laws of every nation since the dawn of history and, until comparatively recently, was punishable in that system of law we have inherited by the penalty of death. The sanctity of an oath may be said to be the very cornerstone of civilization. If men testify falsely when sworn to tell the truth, if public officials violate the oaths they take on assuming office, the result would be the complete collapse not only of all justice but of all government.
>
> In this stance the offense was aggravated in almost every conceivable way. The defendant had a criminal record when he committed the offense. The purpose of his perjury was not only to evade his liability to the United States in huge amounts for taxes due, but also to shield and to protect a condition of indescribable criminality and debauchery. The perjury which was committed before the officer who administered the oath to the

defendant was deliberately repeated on the witness stand in this
court at the trial. In addition to these aggravating circumstances
was the further circumstance that the defendant is the subject of
a foreign power, an alien, who sought to repay the people of the
United States for the welcome they had extended to him and his
family, for the opportunity they had given him and his family,
by violating and defying their laws and by showing in every
possible way his contempt for their institutions.

It is the sentence and judgment of the court that the defendant be committed to the custody of the attorney general and
be by him confined in some institution of the penitentiary type
for a period of four years.

In addition to this four-year sentence for perjury, the judge also
sentenced him to serve three years each on two counts of income
tax evasion and one year on the postal violation charge, all of these
sentences to run concurrently with the sentence on the perjury
charge.

When Pendergast, who was serving his sentence at Leavenworth
Penitentiary, heard that Carrollo had testified that he collected over
half a million dollars annually and turned this money over to Pendergast, he became very angry. He denied having received any
money from Carrollo, except on one occasion when the latter gave
him $60,000.

Carrollo also went to Leavenworth Penitentiary, facing the unpleasant fact that, after he had served his time, he would be subject
to deportation.[2]

Fourteen

Harry and William Rosenberg

W ITH ALL OF THE GRAFT and corruption done by the leaders of the machine, it was but natural that some of the lesser lights should put their fingers in the pie and obtain some of the fruits for themselves. To operate such a well-oiled machine, the persons representing the various cogs had to be in sympathy with the ethics of the leaders. If the leaders believed in and practiced graft and corruption, the others had to help and condone them. To further this, the patronage system was used and the city and county offices were filled with employees who, in gratefulness for the positions given them, would aid the higher-ups.

George Harrington was the Jackson County tax collector, and Jackson County was under domination of Pendergast. Among the deputy collectors employed by Harrington were Harry and William Rosenberg and Robert J. McDermott. Harry Rosenberg, thirty-five years of age, had worked for thirteen years in the office of the tax collector, but his brother William did not enter the employ of the collector until 1933, prior to that time being employed as bookkeeper and teller in several banks.

During his thirteen years of service, Harry Rosenberg noticed how Pendergast took millions of dollars "protecting" fire insurance companies and other enterprises and how Carrollo received his millions protecting gamblers. Why should not he, Harry Rosenberg, protect somebody, of course at a fee. So he evolved a scheme whereby he could also be a protector and thereby increase his wealth.

The laws of the State of Missouri had provided a method for granting relief to property holders in connection with delinquent taxes. The method provided that the property holder petition the county court for an abatement in taxes and, after an examination made by the county counselor and his investigators, the court could grant whatever relief was warranted by the facts disclosed.[1] However, this procedure was lengthy and costly to the taxpayer and seldom did it result in the relief sought, unless, of course, the taxpayer was in the good graces of Pendergast or his henchmen.

Harry Rosenberg saw his opportunity. He would help the tax-payers obtain relief through abatement of taxes. He had noticed that whenever a petition for relief was filed by a taxpayer and it was approved by the county tax collector, the county counselor, possibly out of professional courtesy, would make no investigation, simply also approving it and, with these two approvals, the county court would be certain to grant relief. The only reason that so few reliefs were granted was because Harrington, the county tax collector, rarely approved the petitions, and then only when he had positive knowledge that relief was warranted. It was therefore apparent to Harry Rosenberg that it would be simple to have any petition granted by the court if the approval of the tax collector could be obtained.

For some time Harry Rosenberg practiced writing the name of the tax collector. When he became proficient, he was ready for business. He approached Robert J. McDermott, another deputy collector, and entered into an oral agreement to split any fees received by them in fixing tax abatements.

By soliciting professional tax-fixers these two deputy collectors obtained most of their business. The tax-fixers usually obtained 50 percent of the tax saved by the abatement as their fee and in turn gave Rosenberg from 30 percent to 80 percent of this fee for getting the petition filed, approved, and granted. In addition, Rosenberg also solicited business direct from taxpayers. He approached property owners and urged them to let all their taxes become delinquent. Then he would file petitions for them, approve them by affixing the tax collector's name, and after the court had granted the abatement, collect 50 percent of the taxes thus saved.

Sometimes tax-fixers would object to paying Rosenberg for his efforts, but to these objections Rosenberg would reply, "If you don't like it, we will handle the business through other tax-fixers." Or if some individual property owner objected he would tell him, "If you object, we will not permit any of your tax abatements to go through, and if you are somehow able to secure any abatements, we will nullify them by destroying or losing the granted petitions when they reach this office for preparation of new tax bills."

Rosenberg even went further than this. He would approach property owners who were pursuing legal methods to obtain abatements and tell them that if they did not let him take care of the matter, any abatement granted would be worthless because the petition would be destroyed or conveniently lost before it could reach the taxpayer's hands.

What could the honest citizens do? To get out of their difficulties they had to employ Rosenberg, and thus he began to operate a system which would pay him well. But he did not hesitate to go further. He devised a scheme also to reduce taxes before they became due, by securing reductions in the assessment of real estate. Of course there was only one office in the county which could make a change in the assessment of real estate, and that was the county assessor's office. Rosenberg cultivated John W. Madden, chief deputy assessor of Jackson County, and finally entered into an agreement with him that Rosenberg would furnish Madden with a list of the properties on which assessment reductions were desired, and the latter would effect such reductions through his office. For this service Madden was to receive 50 percent of the fees received by Rosenberg from the property owners whose assessments had been reduced.[2]

Rosenberg, however, disliked to share his fees with anyone. He, therefore, began to double-cross both McDermott and Madden by not sharing his fees with them. There was nothing they could do, because if they complained they would disclose their own offenses. Since McDermott and Madden received none of these fees, they were not involved insofar as income taxes were concerned.

As much as he disliked to share fees with others, Rosenberg also disliked to pay income taxes. His salary as a deputy collector was exempt from federal taxation and only the fees received for the aforementioned tax adjustments would be taxable. For the year 1935 he filed no return. However, for the years 1936, 1937, and 1938 he filed returns, but to aid in reducing his taxes he took into consideration only a portion of these fees and also allegedly entered into a partnership agreement with his brother William, whereby the latter would report one-half of those fees Harry had decided should be reported. Thus the taxes paid by the two brothers were very nominal, surtax rates being avoided.

Special agent Kemp O. Hiatt and internal revenue agent Louis Herman investigated this matter. Their investigation disclosed that Harry Rosenberg had collected fees aggregating $52,192.97 during the four years he operated, of which only about one-half had been reported. However, it was impossible to disprove that a partnership existed, because William Rosenberg corroborated the contention of Harry that such an agreement was in existence. But in thus corroborating his brother's contention, William practically made himself as liable as Harry for the understatement of fees and the evasion of taxes.

The treasury agents discovered that in 1935, when Harry Rosenberg started this racket, he accepted checks, but the following year and thereafter he would only receive payment in currency. In fact, when a taxpayer presented a check in payment of his fee, Rosenberg would get angry and demand that the check be destroyed. He would tell the taxpayer to get a check cashed and to give him the currency, with the remark, "I don't want to leave any trace whereby my name may be linked with this deal."

One amusing incident concerned the Methodist Book Concern of Kansas City. The real estate of this firm, belonging to a charitable institution, was exempt from taxation. But in 1936, Rosenberg through his friend Madden had delinquent assessments made against this firm for the years 1933 to 1936 inclusive, aggregating $4,606.88. Rosenberg or a tax-fixer, Charles M. Spaulding, then approached an officer of this concern. This officer was told that the delinquent taxes must be paid immediately, but that a partial abatement could be obtained by filing a petition.

Later this officer of the company wrote to his superior in New York, and in this correspondence is disclosed the scheme used. An excerpt from this letter reads as follows:

> The authorities have agreed to remove the property from the tax rolls in the future if we would pay one-half of the past due taxes amounting to $2,303.44. . . I hope this meets with your approval. A lawsuit would probably cost us more than $2,300 with the possibility, . . . and one lawyer further says the probability, . . . that our contention would be denied.

Since this concern had been tax exempt for a considerable number of years prior to 1933 and the authorities were willing to remove the property from the tax rolls in the future, why should there be delinquent taxes for the years 1933 to 1936 inclusive? The exemption would be as proper in those years as in the preceding and subsequent years. However, reasoning did not prevail in Kansas City during those years, so the best possible course for the concern was to pay at least one-half and accept a promise that in the future exemption would again be granted.

The New York office of the Methodist Book Concern sent a check in the amount of $2,303.44 payable to the order of George Harrington, tax collector of Jackson County, to the Kansas City office. This check was presented to Spaulding or Rosenberg, but was refused on the ground that it had not been directed to the proper person. The concern then deposited this check in its bank account and drew another check for a like amount payable to Spaulding.

Spaulding testified that Rosenberg received 75 percent of the proceeds of this check.

The officer of the concern wanted to feel secure that the tax bill had been settled and the property removed from the nonexempt tax rolls. So he applied to Rosenberg for some written confirmation of what had been done. He received a letter written on the stationery of the revenue department, Jackson County, stating that the tax on the property of the Methodist Book Concern had been abated in full. This letter was signed "George Harrington, Collector, by Harry Rosenberg, Deputy Collector."

The tax had been abated in full. The county court had abated the taxes against this firm in full, an admission that the property had always been exempt. Thus, the county received no benefit from the payment of $2,303.44 paid by the concern as one-half of the taxes assessed. The only ones who benefited by this payment were Harry Rosenberg and Spaulding.

The facts in this case were presented to the federal grand jury and on July 21, 1939, indictments were returned charging Harry and William Rosenberg with evading income taxes, the former $1,677.48 on three counts for the years 1936, 1937, and 1938, and the latter $380.72 on two counts for the years 1937 and 1938.

They were arraigned on July 26, 1939, pleading not guilty. On October 17, 1939, they both appeared before Federal Judge Otis, William pleading guilty to one count, evasion of income taxes for the year 1937, and Harry to one count, evasion for the year 1936. Acting on these pleas of guilty, Judge Otis sentenced William to serve four months in jail and to pay a fine of $1,000 and Harry to serve six months in jail and fined him $1,500. He modified his sentence so that, if all the taxes, penalties, and fines were paid before November 4, 1939, the jail sentences would be reduced to one and two months, respectively.

Fifteen

Henry F. McElroy

I IN 1926, KANSAS CITY adopted a new charter. One of the charter provisions was that the city would be run by a city manager. The city manager was to be hired by the mayor and the city council, and the tenure of office was to depend on efficiency and good management rather than on politics. Other cities had tried this form of government and found it very satisfactory, but then those cities did not have a machine like Kansas City.

As soon as the charter was adopted the Pendergast-controlled city council hired Henry F. McElroy as city manager. If he had been given a free hand, McElroy would perhaps have become one of the best city managers in the country. What he did do he did efficiently. During the thirteen years he served as city manager he gave Kansas City the finest system of schools and the best fire protection. But his position was dependent upon the political machine, and the politicians had to be satisfied. Pendergast needed money and so did his lieutenants. To obtain this money, gambling, prostitution, and racketeering had to flourish and, to keep these vices flourishing, it was imperative that the police department be kept from interfering. An efficient police department would have done away with the vices. So the police department received instructions to condone the vices. If Carrollo wanted to punish a merchant who refused to pay tribute, or if a Union Station massacre was decided upon by gangster adherents of the machine, it would have been very disconcerting to have the police thwart their efforts.

It was rumored frequently that McElroy and Pendergast were not on the best of terms, and this is possible, because it is believed that the city manager did not condone the conditions existing in Kansas City.

McElroy was born in Amboy, Illinois, August 17, 1865, son of a railroad man who moved to Dunlap, Iowa, to rear his children. By the time he was eleven years old Henry had his first job hauling corncobs at thirty-five cents a day five days a week and on the sixth day his pay was a load of cobs. He also rode a plow horse as winning jockey in races at fairs. He was timekeeper on a railroad construction job and subsequently he ran a store, had a bank, and in 1896, while on his way to the West Coast, he landed in Kansas City. He stayed here and entered the real estate business.

In 1922 he was elected county judge of Jackson County. "Listen," McElroy said when he became judge of the Jackson County court, "I've got $500,000 all my own. I'm going into that court job and give a real business administration."

And he did. He cleaned up the shortages which existed from the court administration given by his predecessor and put the county finances on a sound basis. He made many friends among businessmen who rather liked the idea of the tall beanpole of a county judge being made city manager in 1926 when Kansas City went under the new charter.

Kansas Citians soon found that the man they had hired as city manager should have been called city dictator, although the best that some of the wags could do was to call him the "city damager." The city charter became a machine manifesto and the boys from the precincts who had delivered the vote found the political pari-mutuels were paying dividends. Contractors contracted, supply men supplied, paving progressed, and politicians prospered.

The city manager, with the Yankee twang, the high pockets, the long legs and the white forelock, moved about among the "yesing" councilmen, shaping every action taken. Constantly he employed his "country bookkeeping" to prove that the city was making progress, and his mathematics flew with his sharp pencil as he sold Ten-Year Plan bonds at shrewd prices. He built the thirty-story city hall and the municipal auditorium with those bonds as if the structures were his own, so keen was Judge McElroy that the jobs should be done according to his specifications.

No one ever charged that Judge McElroy in his management of city affairs was doing anything contrary to the law. It was against the new city charter that he was sinning, the sort of sin that, after all, folk argued, was merely the product of his overzealous partisanship.

Typical of Judge McElroy's arrogance was his action in stopping the Walkathon several years ago, an enterprise which popped up about the time the north-side racket leader, the late John Lazia, a machine man, was organizing his forces. The Walkathon managers charged that Lazia was trying to muscle in on their place and chisel part of the take. When someone asked McElroy on what ground he was stopping the Walkathon, he replied it was on "coffee grounds."

He began to pick at the police commissioners early in his administration and, when they asked for their budget to run the police department, Judge McElroy sent them a handsome cut-glass bottle containing castor oil. Judge McElroy rebuffed ministers and others who protested against vice and gambling, advising the women to go home and take care of their children, saying that it was not the police department's part to bring up the children and keep them out of places of vice and gambling. He argued that anybody who would play a slot machine was a fool.

McElroy was ascetic, slender, abstemious as to food, never tasting alcohol, despotic in enforcing his will. He was gentle and benevolent in many and unexpected ways. His temper could flare like a searing flame. But he had been known to stop his car on a busy street and alight to help an old beggar woman safely across.

Many years ago a widower, Judge McElroy cherished his family and his home at 21 West Fifty-seventh Street. It was his pride that, when his wife died and he was left with the care of his small daughter, Mary, and son, Henry F. McElroy, Jr., he had refused to delegate their personal care to anyone else.

"I reared those children myself," Judge McElroy frequently told friends, "because it was my duty. I supervised their baths, their food, their dressing, and their comings and goings. It was my job and no one else could do it."

It was said that he was so interested in his children that he supervised everything they did. He had to approve of their friends and acquaintances and acted as chaperon at any parties given by the young folk.

That was the same spirit Judge McElroy used in ruling the city. He had pride in building the municipal auditorium and the towering thirty-story city hall. His mind evolved the viaducts, the roads, the paving of Brush Creek, the sewers, the Police and Municipal Courts Building, and the airport. He took a proprietary attitude toward these things. He actually carried the keys to many rooms in the municipal auditorium and city hall. He went out to a farm in

Jackson County and selected the trees which later were milled into the finish of the city manager's office.

The files in the office of Chas. O'B. Berry, special agent in charge, Intelligence Unit, Kansas City, contained many anonymous letters alleging that McElroy had received graft payments on almost everything that had been constructed in Kansas City since McElroy took over as city manager.

It was alleged that McElroy had received $50,000 from an unknown source in new $1,000 bills which had been deposited to his bank account. It was said that he received $5,000 a month from the Sanitary Service Company which held the garbage collection contract with the city. He was supposed to have netted $100,000 profit on the purchase by the city of the site for the municipal airport. There were rumors to the effect that McElroy had misappropriated $750,000 of the city's bond money which had been charged as cost of the convention hall site, when in fact it was said that the site had been donated to the city. People said that Judge McElroy had received money from the Ford Motor Company, the Sheffield Steel Company, and the Jones Store Company for settling strikes at those places, and that he had started the strikes so that he could obtain the settlement money.

In fact there were floods of rumors, but not one tangible bit of fact or evidence to use as a starting place for the investigation which had been authorized. Special agent Alfred W. Fleming decided to make a complete study of the judge's life and habits, and used the newspaper clippings maintained in the city newspapers' offices for that purpose. The owners and editors of the *Kansas City Star* and the *Kansas City Journal* cooperated fully in making all files available. While all this was going on, McElroy suddenly resigned as city manager on April 13, 1939.

The investigation of this case was commenced at Kansas City on May 3, 1939, with the cooperation of internal revenue agent John H. Wheeler of the San Francisco division. Internal revenue agents Eugene E. Tobin, Chicago division, Thomas O. Martin, Pittsburgh division, and Bernard P. Fox, Baltimore division, who were assigned on special detail to the office of the special agent in charge, Kansas City, and special agents Roscoe E. Lynn, Arthur M. Clough, Walter E. Rayn, and Herbert P. Holmes, also cooperated in portions of the investigation.

On May 3, 1939, the treasury agents telephoned Judge McElroy's residence, but he refused to talk to them, requesting that the message be delivered to his daughter Mary. He was told that a conference was desired with him with respect to his income tax returns and he was asked to set a time convenient to him, to which he made no reply. On May 4, 1939, McElroy entered St. Mary's Hospital in Kansas City to rest in contemplation of an operation to remove a cataract from his left eye. On June 21, 1939, McElroy returned to his home, where he remained in seclusion without once talking to the treasury agents.

Meanwhile, a plan of campaign had been mapped out and it was decided that, if McElroy had accepted any graft or had made any large profits, it probably would be in real estate or bond deals consummated for the city, since he had proven himself an expert in both of those lines of endeavor. In order to reduce the field of search for bank accounts and safe-deposit boxes, all of the banks and brokerage houses in Kansas City were circularized by mail, with the result that it was learned that McElroy maintained a commercial account and a safe-deposit box at the First National Bank.

The treasury agents never saw the inside of that safe-deposit box, but attention to details finally paid dividends through an analysis of the bank account. Most of the deposit slips contained no information whatsoever, but under date of December 15, 1937, there had been a deposit to McElroy's account in the amount of $3,125 and someone had written on the deposit slip, "50 coupons @ $62.50." So, McElroy did have bonds, and some of the treasury agents concentrated on that angle with interesting results, as will be shown later.

Treasury agents platted out the sites of the city hall, the municipal auditorium, and other projects acquired by the municipality, and interviewed the former owners of the various parcels of real estate. They wanted to know if there had been sales through third parties whereby the price paid by the city could have been increased over the real market value, or if the transferees had paid commissions on said sales, or if the former owners had cut back any of the sales price to anyone. All of the replies were negative.

In almost every instance the former owners were bitter against the shrewd bargaining tactics alleged to have been used by McElroy, who took a keen delight in browbeating the owners and obtaining the property at what was considered bargain prices. In many of these deals McElroy had operated through a realtor known as H. H.

Halvorson, and it was the general opinion that Halvorson had received the commissions on these purchases.

Affairs in Kansas City at that time were in a turmoil, and the treasury agents were fearful that pertinent city records would be destroyed or mislaid where the agents could not find them. However, on the promise of as little publicity as possible, the mayor of Kansas City offered to provide working space in the city hall for the agents and to have the city auditor produce any and all records desired.[1]

An audit of the warrant registers maintained at the city hall disclosed that approximately $150,000 had been paid to Halvorson during a two-year period, ostensibly for services rendered in the acquisition of real estate. Examination of the original warrants revealed that they had, in most instances, been cashed at the First National Bank. Inspection of the income tax returns filed by Halvorson showed that he had not, by any stretch of the imagination, reported as income any sum as revealed by the city warrants.

Halvorson, accompanied by an attorney, visited the office of the Intelligence Unit and, after being placed under oath, was questioned for several days concerning the city warrants made payable to him. He clearly perjured himself by declaring that the entire amount was retained by him and should have been reported by him on his income tax returns.

On about the fourth morning of these interviews, a stranger walked into the office, introduced himself as an attorney just retained by Halvorson, and declared that Halvorson had told him he had perjured himself before the treasury agents and that he now desired to tell the truth.

When granted an opportunity to tell the truth, Halvorson's story was to the effect that he had acted as the confidential agent for the city manager on many real estate transactions. At first, Halvorson had received straight commissions for each deal consummated, but in a short time the volume of business was so great that McElroy indicated that he did not find it convenient to pay the full amount of the commissions as they were earned.

One day Halvorson had been called in to McElroy's office and informed that on the morrow there would be a warrant for a portion of the commissions accruing to Halvorson. When Halvorson called for the warrant, McElroy had two warrants in his possession made payable to Halvorson. McElroy told Halvorson that he needed

$5,000 to short-cut a deal for the city and asked Halvorson to cash one of the warrants and return the proceeds to him. This Halvorson did, and thereafter was content to accept about $12,000 per annum for his services and to cash the other warrants and give the proceeds in cash to McElroy.

After he had purged himself, Halvorson apologized for the trouble he had caused the agents, excusing himself on the grounds that the first attorney who had accompanied him to the Intelligence office was a machine attorney, and Halvorson was afraid that if he told the truth he would be killed. Halvorson was a badly frightened man and, with our knowledge and consent, spent the summer in hiding in the state of Colorado. He is now back in Kansas City enjoying an excellent business.[2]

Halvorson's story was backed up by a mute, but what would have been a damning, piece of evidence. Halvorson had said that, when asked to do so, he would appear at McElroy's office about nine o'clock in the morning where he would receive a warrant which he would cash at the First National Bank. The proceeds would be placed in an envelope and returned to McElroy before noon of the same day. Investigation developed that in every instance McElroy entered his safe-deposit box on the same day that Halvorson cashed city warrants.

One of the more notorious phases of McElroy's country bookkeeping system was a bank account [in the First National Bank] entitled the City Manager's Emergency Fund. Over $6 million flowed through this bank account on which over 4,500 checks were issued. A detailed audit of this account was made by the agents, which was facilitated by reason of the fact that for several years the bank had used the recordak system of bookkeeping which enabled them to see a negative film of the face of the checks issued on said account.

A study of this account convinced the agents that McElroy had used this account as a means of short-cutting procedure at the city hall. Primarily, the account was a clearinghouse for funds which McElroy would borrow from one bond fund and loan to another project where the money was needed. In all cases the borrowed funds were returned when bonds had been sold for the project which had formerly been short of currency.

There was, however, one item in this City Manager's Emergency Fund which led the treasury agents to a $2 million case. A check for $100,000 had been drawn on the fund payable to the Dixie Machinery and Equipment Company, which was one of the favored contracting firms at that time. In tracing that $100,000, the books of the Dixie Company were examined, with the result that a recommendation was made for the assessment of tax and penalties of approximately $2 million. That, however, is another story and will be covered in a subsequent chapter.

On Saturday morning, May 27, 1933, Mary McElroy, daughter of Judge McElroy, was kidnaped from the family residence while taking a bath and held for ransom in the amount of $30,000. Since the banks were closed when the ransom note was received, John Lazia, who was reputed to be king of the muscle men, collected $30,000 from the underworld in Kansas City and delivered the same to Eugene C. Reppert, who at that time was director of police in this city. McElroy paid this money to the kidnapers on Sunday, May 28, 1933, and effected the release of his daughter Mary.

On the next day, Monday, May 29, 1933, Judge McElroy borrowed $30,000 from the First National Bank in Kansas City. It is presumed that McElroy utilized this sum to repay Lazia for the ransom money collected by that individual.

Sometime prior to June 21, 1933, Miss McElroy's kidnapers were apprehended and approximately $16,000 of the ransom money was recovered. It is believed that this recovery was used to reduce McElroy's loan at the First National Bank, because that account was credited with a payment of $16,000 on June 21, 1933, and the balance of $14,000 lay dormant until September 27, 1934, when the loan was paid in full.

Where did that $14,000 come from? The investigation disclosed that it had been withdrawn from some unknown account at the same First National Bank. But the employees interviewed did not know anything about the transaction. The agents were told that the account ledgers at the bank at that time had been divided "A to L" and "M to Z" and that the adding machine tapes indicated that the $14,000 had been withdrawn from an account in the "A to L" group.

There were over thirty thousand accounts in the bank at that time, so the agents were confronted with the dreary prospect of examining about fifteen thousand accounts in the search for a $14,000 withdrawal, which certainly would have entailed weeks of effort with no certainty of success. So, it was decided to try a short-cut. The names of everyone the agents could think of who might have been in a position of paying McElroy that $14,000 were written down and then the ledger accounts for those names were examined.

One of the accounts examined contained a misfiled ledger sheet for E. F. Swinney, chairman of the board of the First National Bank, and on that misfiled ledger sheet was a charge for a withdrawal of $14,000 on September 27, 1934. The "goddess of fortune" had again smiled on the investigators.

When asked to explain this $14,000 transaction, Swinney asked for permission to consult his attorneys, after which he made a statement, the gist of which is as follows:

> As city manager, Mr. McElroy was keeping approximately two or three million dollars of the city's funds at the First National Bank, on which funds no interest was paid. McElroy contended that his daughter had been kidnaped because of his official position as city manager and that, therefore, the balance due on the money borrowed by him to pay the kidnapers was actually city business. McElroy suggested that his friends should do something about paying off the balance. Mr. Swinney discussed this matter with some of the bank officials and it was decided that Mr. Swinney would withdraw that sum from his personal account with which to pay off the balance of McElroy's note in the amount of $14,000, and that Mr. Swinney would be reimbursed by the bank. This was done and, as a result, McElroy did not pay one cent for the release of his daughter. Of the $30,000 paid to the kidnapers, $16,000 was recovered and $14,000 was paid by the bank.

Another interesting angle occurred in the kidnaping of Mary McElroy. When she was released, she apparently had suffered no ill effects and, when the kidnapers were brought to trial, she was not positive in her identification. One of the kidnapers was sentenced to die. When she heard of this, she used all of the influence she could muster, even visiting Governor Park, until she had his sentence commuted to life imprisonment. While the condemned man was in jail in Kansas City, she paid him many visits, bringing him gifts, and continued to do so even after he had been transferred to the penitentiary at Jefferson City. Her reason for being so interested in the welfare of her abductor was never explained satisfactorily.

The testimony received was to the effect that McElroy had accepted money, but what he had done with this money was still a mystery. As previously stated, McElroy had deposited bond coupons to his bank account, and it was therefore assumed that he had purchased bonds. But not one shred of evidence had been uncovered as to the purchase of any bonds by McElroy.

It was believed that the best place for McElroy to purchase bonds without leaving any direct trace would be for him to buy issues authorized by the municipality of Kansas City. Over $30 million of Ten-Year Plan bonds had been sold and the agents were engaged in tracing those transactions through the records at the city hall. But once again the country bookkeeping system was an obstacle, because in certain instances the records disclosed that blocks of bonds had been sold to "private investors," and it seemed impossible to trace either the buyer or the source of the funds used to make said purchases.

There was one bond transaction which was intriguing to the agents. On October 5, 1936, the council of the City of Kansas City had approved the sale of $600,000 of bonds of various issues. The rates of interest to be paid were as high as 3 1/4 percent. However, there were $75,000 of those bonds which only bore interest at the rate of 1 percent, while identical bonds issued the same day paid 2 percent. Who would want to buy those 1 percent bonds? Who was vain enough to desire newspaper publicity that Kansas City issues only paid 1 percent? There was one answer to those questions, and that answer was Judge McElroy. So the agents concentrated on those $75,000 bonds bearing 1 percent.

The director of finance, Kansas City, stated that all original issues of bonds sold by that municipality were delivered to the purchasers by him upon receipt of a certified check or other evidence of value for which reason it was not the customary practice to accept receipts for the delivery of bonds. The director asserted that the records in his office would not disclose the name or identity of the person or persons who had purchased the heretofore mentioned $75,000 in bonds. When closely questioned the director did state that he had received the payment for the bonds on October 1, 1936.

Investigation disclosed that the said bonds had been delivered to the City of Kansas City by the lithographer on October 10, 1936. Armed with this information, the agents again confronted the director of finance and asked him how he could have delivered the bonds on October 1 when in fact they had not been in his possession until the tenth of the same month. It was also intimated that it was believed the city had not received any payment whatsoever for the said bonds. The fear of the sequence of that intimation broke through the veil of the country bookkeeping system. The director of finance started the inside machinery to working, with the result that the city treasurer produced a memorandum showing that payment for said bonds had been received from the First National Bank on October 1, 1936.

The agents encountered a really clever cover-up scheme. The records at the First National Bank failed to disclose that the said bonds were purchased by that bank either for its own account or for the account of a client. However, the cashier's check register at that bank did disclose that on October 1 a cashier's check payable to Maurice Carey, city treasurer, had been issued in the amount of $75,000, but the name of the purchaser of said check was not shown on the records.

Investigation in the deep and dusty files of the First National Bank disclosed that on October 1, 1936, some person delivered $75,000 in currency to the said bank for which a "credit teller's account" memorandum was made out by paying teller Horace Hamm. As a bookkeeping offset teller, Hamm also prepared a "debit teller's account" memorandum which was used to pay for the heretofore mentioned cashier's check. Hamm and other bank officials were closely questioned regarding these entries, but they stoutly maintained that they had no recollection of the transaction or the identity of the person who had brought the $75,000 to the bank. Someone with a sound knowledge of banking practice had conceived this scheme which covered up the trail completely.

There is an axiom in the strategy of war to the effect that if a position cannot be taken by frontal attack, see if it can be taken from the rear. So, a devious route was tried which produced interesting results.

It was learned from an informer that there was a young bond salesman in Kansas City who was reported to have a prodigious memory and who was reported to be a wizard at remembering bond issues, prices, and the names of persons who had purchased bonds. This young man had at one time been employed by the bond department of a bank and, being interested in municipal issues, had made it his business to know all about such issues. In fact he had been so successful that he had left the employ of the bank to start his own business selling municipal bond issues. The informer cautioned the agents that this young man was sympathetic toward the machine and, if he was questioned directly and to the point, nothing of interest would be gained. On the other hand, he was known to like to brag about his accomplishments.

It appeared to be questionable whether this person would know anything about bonds purchased by McElroy, but the agents decided to take a chance. Without revealing his identity, one of the agents struck up a casual acquaintanceship with this bond salesman. A willingness to listen and a little flattery on the part of the agent aided the cause and the young man became engaged in relating anecdotes of his experiences in selling bonds. Casually, the agent brought the name of McElroy into the conversation, praising the former city manager's ability and the difficulty most people had in transacting business with him.

The young bond salesman replied that other salesmen might have had difficulties with McElroy, but that he had consummated a deal through Judge McElroy and had done it quickly and easily. "Why," he said, "I remember one time the city sold at private sale $75,000 in bonds bearing 1 percent interest. While I was employed at the City National Bank and Trust Company, I found that one of my clients was interested in buying those bonds. So I went to Judge McElroy and told him I had an offer for those issues at $97 plus accrued interest, but since I did not know who owned the bonds, I wanted him to help me try and close the deal. The Judge told me to come back in a few days and he would let me know. When I returned, the judge stated that he had contacted the owners of the bonds and they would accept the offer." The bond salesman continued, "The judge instructed me to have a draft prepared in the name of M. W. Small for the full amount, deliver the draft to the judge and he would turn over the bonds to me." "So," the salesman continued, "I went back to the office, had a cashier's check prepared and the next day the deal was consummated."

The agent was astounded by this story. Out of a clear sky the bond salesman friend had picked out the one deal for which the agents were looking. The goddess of luck was still with the agents. The trail was hot again. Attacked by investigational fever, the tempo increased. The days did not seem long enough. Down to the City National Bank and Trust Company the agents went. Yes, there was a cashier's check made payable to M. W. Small in an amount approximating $73,000 and on the reverse thereof an endorsement showing it had cleared through the First National Bank on June 2, 1937.

Back to the First National Bank and into their records again. For what had the check been used? The records in the bond department of that bank revealed that under date of May 23, 1937, an order had been placed for the purchase of $75,000 face value U.S. Treasury bonds, 2 1/2 percent, 1949 to 1953, at a price of 98 1/32. Those bonds were requested in $5,000 denominations and were for the account of M. W. Small.

Who was M. W. Small? How had the bonds been paid for? Who had received the bonds? No one at the bank knew, or at least they would not tell. But the mute adding machine tapes of the bond department did give the lead needed. The cost of those U.S. Treasury bonds was $74,393.23. They had been paid for with two items, one in the exact amount of the heretofore mentioned cashier's check issued by the City National Bank and by an item of $1,143.23. A scrutiny of Judge McElroy's account at the First National Bank showed that it had been charged on June 3, 1937, for a withdrawal of $1,143.23. Our reconstruction of these facts disclosed that Judge McElroy had at least paid for a portion of the cost of the U.S. Treasury bonds and that delivery of the same had taken place on or about June 3, 1937.

It was decided to go over the heads of all the officials of the First National Bank to lay the problem before the chairman of the board of that institution, who said that he would see to it that the officers of the bank cooperated, and issued orders to that effect.

The bond clerk at the First National Bank, advised by the chairman of the board to tell the truth, testified to the effect that he had been ordered by one of the vice-presidents to bring the hereinabove-mentioned $75,000 face value U.S. Treasury bonds into one of the private offices maintained at the bank, where the bonds were delivered to Judge McElroy in the presence of the bond clerk and the vice-president. The judge signed a receipt with the name M. W. Small for the delivery of the bonds. Now the agents had testimony to the effect that Judge McElroy had accepted money from Halvorson and they now knew of the purchase and sale of Kansas City municipal bonds and the use of the proceeds thereof to acquire U.S. Treasury bonds. The only thing that remained was to show the present whereabouts or ownership of those bonds and, knowing the serial numbers of the bonds, they were able to do that.

During this investigation the agents were contacted by Judge McElroy's son, Henry McElroy, Jr., who very likely was operating in a liaison capacity for his father. Henry informed them that his father was keeping in close touch with the investigation they were making through information supplied by persons in Kansas City. Henry was convinced of his father's innocence and stated that he was attempting to have his father meet with the treasury agents and answer any questions which might be asked.

On one of those visits Henry stated that he had talked about tax matters to his father and they had discovered that his father had not filed gift tax returns covering certain gifts made by the judge to his children, Mary and Henry. Henry declared that they had remedied that deficiency by filing delinquent gift tax returns just a few days previous to that conversation and paying a gift tax of approximately $12,000.

When questioned regarding the nature of the gifts, Henry stated that they had consisted of cash, real estate, stock, and bonds. The son submitted in his own handwriting a list of the assets, including the serial numbers of the bonds, and sure enough, the treasury bonds given to Mary and Henry by their father, Judge McElroy, bore the identical serial numbers as the bonds that had been traced as having been purchased through the name of M. W. Small.

The receipt of money from Halvorson and the income from bonds had not been reported by McElroy. It was disclosed that for the period 1933 to 1936, inclusive, McElroy had failed to report $274,263.15 received by him as income upon which additional taxes in an amount of $62,326.27 were due.

The facts and evidence were presented to Maurice M. Milligan, U.S. district attorney, who decided to present the case to the grand jury. On September 14, 1939, subpoenas were issued, requiring witnesses to appear before the grand jury on September 18, 1939. However, witnesses were never required to testify. On September 15, 1939, McElroy died at his home of uremia and heart disease. He had appealed his case to a higher court.

Within a year his daughter Mary followed her father to the grave, a suicide.

Sixteen

Otto P. Higgins

T O   F U R T H E R   I T S   O W N   E N D S , the machine had to dominate the police department. The police had to be amenable to the wishes and desires of the politicians. The sources from which graft came, namely, gambling, prostitution, racketeering and "muscling" into prosperous enterprises, had to be protected against interference by peace officers. So, to guide the police in the furtherance of these objects, the director of police had to be one of the "gang."

Eugene C. Reppert was made director of police. Under his regime crime really flourished, but as a result of the Union Station massacre on June 17, 1933, he was indicted by a grand jury for perjury in denying that he had instructed his subordinates to "lay off" the Union Station case, telling them, "This is not our case; it is a government case. Go on about your assignments." He resigned his position.

Otto Higgins on April 15, 1934, was appointed director of police by members of the city council and upon the advice of McElroy, although Pendergast never liked him. Along with Reppert, Thomas J. Higgins, chief of detectives, and Lieutenant George Rayen, head of the police motor car theft bureau, were indicted for perjury, but Otto Higgins would not suspend them, describing them as good officers, and the Pendergast-controlled city council rejected a resolution to call for their suspension.

Otto Higgins was born at Streator, Illinois, on January 19, 1890. He is the only child of his parents, who brought him to Kansas City, Kansas, while still a youngster. His late father was a boilermaker for the Missouri Pacific Railroad Company. As a youth Otto obtained a position as janitor for a bank and thus assisted in paying his school expenses. After graduating from the University of Kansas, he became a police reporter for the *Kansas City Star.* This newspaper sent him to France during the World War as a war correspondent and he remained overseas for fourteen months. Returning, he obtained a law degree and was admitted to the Missouri bar in 1920. He then engaged in legal practice until his appointment as director of police.

On January 11, 1911, he married. To that union there were born three children, one son, who died in July 1939 while the father was under investigation, and two daughters, both now married.

Higgins carried on as director of police where his predecessor had left off, only that Higgins put the corruption of his department on a more efficient plane. Each police captain was required to list accurately all the prostitutes within his district and this list was used to determine whether these districts collected sufficient protection money from them. Thus the machine was assured of a steady income from this source.

Carrollo took care of the gamblers, but he had to work with the police department. He was a welcome, frequent, and privileged caller at the office of Higgins and sometimes the latter even sent for him. Orders were given to the office attendants that Carrollo was never to be kept waiting and that he was to have immediate access to the director's inner private office. He was often referred to as the unofficial chief of police. Higgins resigned as director of police on April 15, 1939.

It will be recalled that on April 28, 1939, Edward L. Schneider, appearing before a federal grand jury, received permission from Pendergast to tell the truth and that he did testify to matters which affected the income tax liability of Pendergast. He promised to visit the office of the Intelligence Unit on May 1, 1939, to give some further information, but instead he disappeared on that day, his machine being found on a bridge spanning the Missouri River and his body was recovered from that river several days later. Did Schneider commit suicide and if so, why?

It was learned that early on the morning of May 1, 1939, Higgins visited Schneider. He did not enter the house but talked to Schneider in his automobile in front of the house. After this conversation, Schneider's automobile was found on the bridge, certain papers which he was to bring to the treasury agents wrapped up in a bundle on the seat of the car. As he left his home and prior to his conversation with Higgins, Schneider told his wife that he would be at the office of the Intelligence Unit and suggested that if she desired to contact him to call that office. In spite of the fact that he told his wife where she could reach him and in spite of the fact that he took with him a bundle containing important records, all of which indicates as he left his home he intended visiting the office of the treasury agents, he, after the conversation with Higgins, disappeared into the murky waters of the Missouri River. According to Higgins, his only reason for paying such an early visit to Schneider's home was to cheer up the latter.

Special agent R. C. Lynn and internal revenue agent B. P. Fox were assigned to investigate the income tax liability of Higgins. Special agent Alfred W. Fleming also cooperated in the investigation.

They discovered that between 7:40 A.M. and 8:00 A.M. on the morning of May 1, 1939 (about the time Higgins held his conversation with Schneider), Higgins telephoned to W. C. Watson, chief of the audit section, Sixth Internal Revenue Collection District of Missouri, Kansas City. Watson was at home when he received the call. Higgins asked him whether he was sure he would be in his office that morning. Watson replied in the affirmative. Between 9:30 A.M. and 9:45 A.M. that morning, Higgins, accompanied by Elmer B. Hodges, visited Watson at his office for about an hour. (During this time Schneider's automobile was found on Fairfax Bridge.) During the visit Higgins stated that he was filing amended income tax returns for the years 1934, 1936, 1937, and 1938, and a delinquent return for the year 1935. Watson later learned that while his visitors were in his office, Albert F. Hillix, an associate of Hodges, filed the returns and paid the additional taxes. After leaving Watson, Higgins and Hodges visited with others in the collector's office. They left the collector's office about 11:00 A.M.

Meanwhile the treasury agents began delving into the financial transactions of Higgins. His annual salary as director of police was exempt from federal taxation, but they found that he was spending almost four times as much a year as his annual salary. The first item of income found by the agents was that Carrollo was paying Higgins $1,000 a month for the protection of the gamblers. Small wonder that Carrollo was such a privileged caller at Higgins's office. This item had not been included on his amended income tax returns, therefore, even the amended returns were false. The treasury agents were to find more income which had not been reported.

After Schneider's death, which shocked all of Kansas City, especially the employees of the various Pendergast-controlled firms, new disclosures came to light. The mysterious actions of Higgins caused much speculation, and some of the employees of these firms came to the treasury agents asking for protection. One such employee visited the hotel room of one of the treasury agents and pleaded that he be allowed to remain overnight, explaining that he was afraid to go home. Another employee, who had a wife and two children, hired a bodyguard. Everything was in a turmoil, but one thing was certain, the employees would now cooperate with the treasury agents.

The books of the Pendergast-controlled corporations were audited and, with the help of the employees, it was disclosed that at least $500,000 had been diverted from them to persons unknown. In some instances, fictitious invoices were used, charged to purchases or expenses on the books of the corporations, and the checks of the corporations in payment of these fictitious invoices were cashed. In other instances, certain sales of the corporations were not entered on the books and, when payments for these sales were made, the checks were cashed. Thus the net income of the corporations over a twelve-year period was understated in excess of $500,000, consisting of understated sales and overstated expenses. Who got this money? When Pendergast, who was at that time in Leavenworth Penitentiary, heard of the looting of his corporations, he was furious. At least 50 percent of this money belonged to him as principal stockholder. He ordered that accounting firms be employed to work with the treasury agents to gather all the facts.

It was preposterous. Here were corporations controlled by Pendergast, who was the dictator of Kansas City and who exacted tribute from others, paying tribute to someone else. Pendergast denied getting the money, employees of the corporations swore neither Pendergast nor Schneider got it, and the estate of Schneider bore mute testimony that at least he had not retained it. Pendergast did not have to use such subterfuge to get money from his own firms. His method was to have money withdrawn as dividends in the name of Schneider. But, if neither Pendergast nor Schneider got the money, who did get it and why? Did the corporations controlled by the dictator have to pay tribute to others?

If so, this calls to mind an ancient axiom which reads as follows: "Great fleas have little fleas upon their backs to bite 'em, and little fleas have lesser fleas, and so ad infinitum."

An examination of the checks issued to pay the fictitious purchases and expenses disclosed that most of these checks were endorsed and cashed by Schneider, but during four years at least
checks aggregating $48,000 had been endorsed and cashed by Hig-
gins. What Schneider had done with the cash he thus obtained
could not be ascertained since his lips had been sealed by death,
but one of the bookkeepers, who had prepared the checks thus
cashed by Schneider, said that on one occasion Schneider, very
much worried, had remarked that it was difficult to keep them all
satisfied and still keep the boss from finding out about it. He had
not paid much attention to this remark at the time it was made, but
with the revelations now in progress, his opinion now was that
Schneider, under duress, had to pay tribute to others and had to
keep the payment of it from Pendergast.

Higgins, however, was in a different situation. The checks bore
mute testimony that he had received one of these payments. When
first interviewed, he denied ever having received any money from
Schneider or the corporations, but when he learned that the treasury agents had discovered the checks endorsed and cashed by
him, he voluntarily came to see the agents. He explained that he
had been authorized by Pendergast to act as "official greeter" to
welcome visitors to Kansas City, and that Pendergast had told him
that any expenses he incurred in this official capacity would be refunded to him by Schneider. He admitted receiving money from
Schneider and identified the checks received.

His story that Pendergast told him to get his expenses as official
greeter from the corporations was considered ridiculous. In the first
place, Pendergast needed practically every cent he could get his
hands on to satisfy his gambling needs and, in the second place,
why should Pendergast be responsible for an expense benefiting
the city, when such an expense easily could be borne by the city, especially since the city council and the city executives were under
his domination and would pass every bill he desired. No one could
recall that Higgins had exclusively entertained anyone visiting
Kansas City. He did, of course, meet distinguished visitors, but no
more than did other city executives.

Pendergast when interviewed in the hospital at Leavenworth
Penitentiary became more and more incensed when he heard Higgins had obtained some of the missing money of his corporations.

After he had heard the explanation Higgins had given, he denied that he had ever told anyone to be an official greeter and ended his tirade with, "You can bring Otto Higgins in this hospital room and I will denounce him as a liar and a rat."

One of the corporation checks endorsed and cashed by Higgins was payable to the Police Horse Show and Sportsmen's Exposition, an affair given by the Police Benefit Association, an organization instituted for the relief of widows and orphans of policemen who died in the service. Higgins admitted cashing this check for $100 and retaining the currency for his own use. As one newspaper put it, "Fine Guy. Taking money from widows and orphans."

Needless to say, this money received from Schneider was not reported either on his original or amended returns.

The treasury agents found more and more unreported income. It was disclosed that he received interest on bank deposits, notes and bonds, rental income from four parcels of real estate, and that he used large sums of currency for expenditures.

In addition it was discovered by the treasury agents that he used the police department for whatever work he thought necessary, even if it was for personal use. Thus it was found that five policemen, one a sergeant, paid by the city for their services, actually worked on the personal property of Higgins, his cottage at 3221 East Thirty-second Street, his palatial summer home at Lake Lotawana, and his farms at Circleville, Kansas. They painted and repaired buildings, installed tile bathrooms, built roads, and took care of the yards and the grass. Higgins did not pay them anything, their salaries being paid by the city for services allegedly rendered as protectors of the citizens from the lawless element. Some of the citizens knew what was going on, but they did not dare to object, although, while the crew was redecorating and remodeling Higgins's home, someone put a sign on the lawn at night, reading, "This work is being done by city employees." One of the crew later testified, "That sign sure burned Otto up and he didn't waste any time tearing it down."

Most of the crew testified readily, but one of them was afraid to talk. He was not quite ready to believe that Kansas City was being brought back under the Constitution and that free speech was again a part of the fundamental law in Kansas City. He staunchly denied that he had painted the buildings of Higgins at Lake

Lotawana. When one of the agents asked him, "Are you sure you did not even help paint the house?" he replied, "Sure, I painted the boathouse."

Higgins explained how the road leading from the highway to his palatial summer home was built by policemen by naively stating, "Why, you see, a bunch of the boys used to just sort of drop out for a visit and, of course, they wanted to show their appreciation and just naturally pitched in to help at anything they saw that needed attention."

Detective Sergeant Charles E. Zans, an expert tile setter, told a different story, however. While awaiting a shipment of tile to be used in the bathroom of Higgins's home, he had an opportunity to earn $100 setting tile in two new dwellings. Zans said, "I could have done it before the other tile got here. I went to Higgins and told him it was a chance to make $100 if he would let me off. Higgins replied, 'Hell, no. If you haven't anything to do, go down to my farm at Circleville and work there until the tile gets there.' So Bud Shoemaker [Higgins's police chauffeur] drove me down." Meanwhile the citizens of Kansas City were paying Zans to render service as a sergeant of police.

He also used John O'K. Taussig, a policeman in the inspection division and a former U.S. deputy collector, to determine whether his original income tax returns were under investigation. This occurred in March 1939, when it was first publicly learned that Pendergast and O'Malley were under investigation. He had previously sent Taussig to Washington in an attempt to have the prosecutions for vote frauds stopped. He sent him to Chicago, where Taussig claimed to have contacts, in an attempt to determine the status of Higgins as to income tax investigations. He did not obtain any information, but did suggest to Higgins that, if his returns were not correct, he had better file amended ones.

Taussig also told he obtained an extension of time for Higgins in filing his 1938 return because Higgins was too busy to file before March 15, 1939. It may be recalled that on March 13, 1939, Higgins left for Washington in a desperate attempt to have the grand jury investigation of Pendergast's and O'Malley's income tax liabilities stopped.

It is significant that Higgins filed amended returns only after Schneider had started to tell the truth, but Schneider died before he was able to tell about the activities of Higgins. Perhaps Schneider could have told much more than was actually discovered by the treasury agents.

The investigation disclosed that during the five years, 1934 to 1938 inclusive, Higgins had a gross income of $109,627.75, of which his salary as director of police, $25,133.28, was exempt from federal taxation. The balance, $84,494.47, represented payments received from Carrollo and Schneider, interest and rental income, and tribute exacted from prostitutes and saloonkeepers. Of this sum he had reported only $24,331.57 and had evaded income taxes in an amount of $5,970.12.

He was indicted on October 26, 1939, on four counts of evasion of income taxes (1934 to 1938 inclusive), and on November 3, 1939, pleaded guilty to counts three and four, counts one and two being nolle prossed. Federal Judge John Caskie Collet sentenced him to serve two years in the penitentiary on count three and to five years probation on count four, the probationary period to begin after the prison sentence was completed. He was taken the same day to Leavenworth Penitentiary.[1]

Seventeen

Dixie Machinery and Equipment Company, Boyle-Pryor Construction Company, Missouri Asphalt Products Company, John J. Pryor, William D. Boyle (Deceased)

T HE INVESTIGATION OF THESE CASES was begun at Kansas City on June 29, 1939, by special agent Alfred W. Fleming with the cooperation of internal revenue agents John H. Wheeler, of the San Francisco division, Eugene E. Tobin, Chicago division, and Thomas O. Martin, Pittsburgh division, who were assigned on special detail to the office of the special agent in charge, Kansas City. Special Agent Herbert P. Holmes also cooperated in portions of the investigation.

While the treasury agents were investigating the notorious City Manager's Emergency Fund, which was a commercial bank account maintained by H. F. McElroy, formerly city manager of Kansas City, to short-cut city business and through which approximately $6 million of city funds flowed, they found that the said account had been charged for a withdrawal in the amount of $100,000. Due to the fact that the bank used the recordak system of bookkeeping, we were enabled to see a negative film of the face of the check and thereby learned that the same had been made payable to the Dixie Machinery and Equipment Company.

In an endeavor to trace the recipient of this $100,000, the treasury agents requested the Dixie Machinery and Equipment Company, as a third party to the McElroy investigation, to produce its books and records for inspection. The record produced was a cash journal which was maintained in a single-entry method of bookkeeping. That is, the cash receipts were entered on the left side of the book and the disbursements were recorded on the opposite page.

They found the $100,000 recorded therein, the entry being identi-
fied merely with a letter "L." The company's auditor explained that
the letter signified that the amount was a loan and was not therefore reported as income on the corporation's income tax return. A
quick scrutiny of the cash journal revealed that there were several
sizable receipts identified as loans, but the startling fact was that
there were no withdrawals entered on the book as being repayment
of the said loans.

The company's auditor convinced the agents that the $100,000
they were tracing had been deposited in the firm's bank account,
and they departed, but not before they had made notes of several of
the receipt items marked "loans."

The Dixie Company had been described in the local newspapers
as a politically favored corporation under the control of John J.
Pryor, a close friend of Pendergast for many years. Convinced that
the Dixie Company had received many thousands of dollars from
the city for the rental of construction equipment, the agents decided
to investigate those loan items. They proceeded to the city hall and
started to search the warrant registers maintained there. Those
records revealed that some six or seven of the loan items that had
been noted in the rapid search of the Dixie books were in fact payments to that corporation for services rendered the city. Upon receipt of this information the commissioner of internal revenue
authorized a complete investigation of the affairs of the Dixie Machinery Company and its related corporations.

According to the *Kansas City Star,* John J. Pryor rose from the status of saloonkeeper to a partnership in construction companies into
which was siphoned millions of dollars of tax money for the benefit
of the favored Pendergast machine leaders.

As boss of the fifth precinct of the first ward, where Pendergast
and O'Malley had their start, beginning about forty years ago,
Pryor believed in defending his sovereignty with his fists, or sometimes with a gun if it were necessary. In March 1900, Pryor fired
several shots at a group of canvassers who appeared at his saloon
to check alleged fraudulent registrations in the rooming house
above the saloon. He was arrested, but friends in court protected
him as they were to do on subsequent occasions. Pryor was arrested several times from 1900 until 1908, at least once for operating
a gambling game on a Missouri River excursion boat. Once, on
a New Year's Eve, he was taken into custody for carrying a loaded

revolver, but explained that he merely wanted to fire it to celebrate the New Year.

Pryor's most serious brush with the law came in November 1906, when he was charged with the murder of George Morton, a cook. Police obtained signed statements from twelve witnesses who said they saw Pryor strike Morton as he stood on Walnut Street near the Pryor saloon. The cook fell and was killed when he struck his head on the curb. The case of the state versus Pryor for the murder of Morton rivaled the notorious Charles Gargotta case for delays and legal pettifogging.[1] After several trials Pryor was finally acquitted in September 1911.

Pryor's political progress was uninterrupted by his trials for murder. He continued to solidify his political power and frequently boasted that he always had and always would run his precinct to suit himself. Some dental boys put a big dent in Pryor's reputation for toughness in 1916, in an incident that was relished by opponents and others who had been bullied by Pryor. A man by the name of O. R. Six, a dental student, and several friends appeared in a polling place where Pryor made an insulting remark about a colored handkerchief in one of the men's pockets. The fight was on. Pryor asked for Six and got him. In a moment Pryor's 250 pounds were on the sidewalk. Pryor reached for his hip pocket and a shot was heard. A policeman appeared, the fighters disappeared, and so did the policeman. Pryor was carried home and tucked in bed. It is said that Pendergast appeared soon after the fight and met Six. "I don't see how I ever overlooked you," the boss said. It wasn't until the next day that word got around that Six had lasted eleven rounds against Jim Flynn, the fellow that knocked out Jack Dempsey.[2]

With the Pendergast machine firmly entrenched in power, Pryor entered the construction field in partnership with the late William D. Boyle. The companies headed by Boyle and Pryor vied with Pendergast's Ready Mixed Concrete Company in getting big slices out of Kansas City's Ten-Year Plan bond funds. Boyle and Pryor shared equally in the ownership of these companies, and all profits were divided between them on an equal basis.

The plan of campaign mapped out by the treasury agents in this case was simplified by the fact that it was known that at least one of the Pryor companies had failed to report as income amounts received for services rendered to the municipality of Kansas City. So they commenced the audit at the source and made a complete survey of the warrant registers at the city hall to ascertain the total sum of the monies paid to the Pryor companies by the said municipality.

Armed with that information, an audit of the books of account of the Pryor firms was made and it was found that from the year 1934 to 1938, inclusive, the Dixie Company had failed to report on its tax returns as gross income an amount approximating $750,000 received from the city for rental of machinery and for other services. In one year alone the Dixie Company had received over $150,000 gross income from that source and had failed to include a single penny of said amount on its income tax return.

Certain of the warrants representing those payments bore the endorsement of Wm. D. Boyle. Those warrants were cashed and no entry for the receipt thereof was made on the corporation's books of account. Other warrants received were deposited to the corporation's credit in a local bank and the receipt was recorded on the books of account, but omitted from its tax returns. Other warrants were recorded on the taxpayer's books as loans.

In addition to the omission of this gross income, it was also discovered that during the years under investigation there had been deducted on the tax returns of the corporations owned and controlled by Messrs. Pryor and Boyle over $900,000 represented in most instances by checks made payable to cash. Those checks had been cashed without endorsement. The audit revealed that, prior to the advent of the Social Security tax, a substantial portion of said cash checks had been charged to payroll expense, but after the date the said tax became effective, the charges to payroll ceased and the cash checks were then charged to purchases of materials and supplies.[3]

It appeared that not only was the gross income understated, but the expenses had been overstated, both aiding in reducing the net income of the corporations. The omission of gross income was not difficult to prove, since the city warrants proved the payment for services rendered and also the disposal of the proceeds of the warrants, but it was not so easy to ascertain what had become of the proceeds of the checks made payable to cash. It was evident, however, that the corporation had claimed false deductions in charging these checks to payroll or merchandise expenses.

An analysis of these cash checks disclosed that each week from four to six checks were drawn in odd amounts which, when added together, always totaled exactly $4,000. Examination of the checks revealed that many of them had been held for months before being cashed and that, in fact, some of the checks drawn as early as September 1935 had been cashed at a local bank during the month of February 1936.

The bookkeeper of the corporations testified that years ago Pryor had instructed her to prepare several checks each month payable to cash in odd amounts which would amount to an even $4,000 and that she had done this each month, using her own ingenuity as to the odd amounts to be used on the checks, always giving the checks to Pryor. At first she had been instructed by him to charge these checks to payroll expense, this method being the one most expedient, because an ordinary audit would not reveal the "pads." The corporations had so many employees, chiefly laborers, and the personnel changed so often that it would be difficult for an auditor making a cursory examination to prove the payroll overstated. She said that after the Social Security law went into effect and it was necessary to report the wages paid to the hired help, this practice was discontinued, since the payroll expense had to agree with the wages reported on the Social Security returns. She was therefore instructed thereafter to charge these checks drawn to cash to various merchandise expense accounts, but that the practice of drawing several checks for odd amounts always aggregating $4,000 per month was continued. She said that she had no vouchers or statements to substantiate these items entered upon the books as expense.

On June 3, 1938, Boyle was killed by a bolt of lightning while watching a tournament on a local golf course, and from then on Pryor alone managed the affairs of the corporations.

The investigation showed that on February 7, 1936, 189 of the checks, some drawn as early as September 1935, had been cashed at a local bank in the total amount of $130,000. The checks had not been endorsed and no one at the bank could remember the identity of the person or persons cashing the same. The bank officials were evidently attempting to shield Pryor, who was one of their best and most influential customers.

The records of the bank disclosed that on February 6, 1936, the bank had ordered $150,000 in new $1,000 bills from the Federal Reserve Bank and that the Brinks Express Company had made the delivery. On February 6, 1936, the Brinks Express Company picked up $20,000 of these new $1,000 bills from the bank and returned them to the Federal Reserve Bank. Thus, the bank had needed only $130,000 of the new $1,000 bills on February 7, 1936, the day on which $130,000 worth of checks of Pryor's corporations had been cashed. The bank officials were still unable to remember the identity of the persons receiving this money.

Later it was disclosed, however, that certain of these $1,000 bills, identified by the serial numbers obtained from the records of the Federal Reserve Bank and the Brinks Express Company, were deposited in the bank accounts of Pryor and Boyle.

In this manner, by obtaining the proceeds of warrants payable to the corporations, without entering the gross income on the books of the corporations, and by obtaining the proceeds of checks drawn to each which were charged to expenses of the corporation, it was possible for Pryor and Boyle to receive large sums of money belonging to the corporations. Thus the corporations, by understating gross income and overstating of expenses, were able to reduce their net income and, since the records of the corporations did not disclose the identity of the persons to whom the money went, Pryor and Boyle were able to omit the receipt of this money on their personal income tax returns.

It was also discovered that Pryor and Boyle had purchased large amounts of U.S. Treasury bonds from this bank, using funds from an unknown source. One purchase amounting to $24,783.13 was found to have been purchased with checks issued by the Pryor corporations, the checks being charged to operating expenses of the corporations. When the serial numbers of the bonds were obtained, it was disclosed that practically one-half of them were part of the estate of Boyle. As stated previously, Boyle and Pryor divided all profits equally.

At the start of this investigation the treasury agents arrived at Pryor's office one morning and prepared to depart for luncheon at about noon of that first day, whereupon Pryor most cordially expressed his appreciation for their having completed the examination in such a short time. When informed that they would return after lunch, Pryor said, "Hell, I guess you guys are just starting, and here I thought you were finished."

In view of Pryor's reputation for toughness, it was decided to try to soften him and, with that in view, he was told from time to time of the glaring errors discovered on the books of his corporations.

One day Pryor called the agents into his office and told them that from then on he would not talk. His creed had been one of fists and not conversation. He intended to live up to his teachings and advised the agents that under no circumstances would he answer any questions that might be asked. Pryor had only one favor to ask, and that was, would the agents, if possible, leave Mrs. Pryor out of the investigation?

He was told that, if the agents could see their way clear to do so, they would not interrogate Mrs. Pryor and, in return, they asked Pryor's full cooperation in producing the books, records, and canceled checks of the corporations, which he did, but he still stuck to his decision not to answer questions. On one occasion the firm's auditor said he could not find the canceled checks for a certain two years. This was mentioned to Pryor, and within two hours the missing checks were delivered to the Intelligence Unit office.

The final softening process came when Pryor was called into the Intelligence Unit office for the purpose of obtaining a statement from him. Pryor stood on his constitutional rights, but for three days he was shown item after item and merely asked, "What explanation do you have for this?" Pryor never talked to the extent of giving any information, his answers being, "I don't know." But it seems that during those three days Pryor and his attorney became convinced that they could not successfully maintain a defense against the government's case.

The facts secured in this investigation were presented to a federal grand jury at Kansas City on November 28, 1939, and subsequent dates. On December 1, 1939, an indictment containing nine counts was returned charging Pryor with attempted evasion of income taxes of the Boyle-Pryor Construction Company for the years 1934 to 1937, inclusive, of the Dixie Machinery and Equipment Company for the year 1934, of the Missouri Asphalt Products Company for the year 1935, and of his personal income taxes for the years 1934, 1935, and 1937. The total amount of income not reported was over $2.7 million, upon which additional taxes aggregating over $1 million were due.

On January 13, 1940, Pryor pleaded guilty to three counts of the indictment. He was sentenced to two years in a federal penitentiary, fined $20,000 and, in addition thereto, was placed on probation for five years after the expiration of his prison sentence.

On January 20, 1940, Pryor entered the federal penitentiary at Leavenworth. Arriving by motor car, he walked up the long flight of steps alone, his chin in his collar. A cold wind swept across the front of the prison. He did not look back before passing through the gate.

Some of the income not reported by Pryor came from the Rathford Engineering Company. Since this matter involved several others, no mention has been made of it in this chapter. Another interesting angle which has not been discussed in this chapter relates to the finding of some of the government bonds purchased by Pryor in the possession of Matthew S. Murray. These matters will be discussed in the following two chapters.

Eighteen

Rathford Engineering Company

T HE AFFAIRS OF THIS pseudo firm constitute one of the interesting stories that came to light when the Pendergast machine began to totter. An awakened citizenry, led by the *Kansas City Star* and *Times* newspapers, began to uncover all kinds of corruption in the civic affairs of Kansas City. Meanwhile, the treasury agents were always uncovering something new. One investigation just led into another one. The records of McElroy disclosed the payments to the Dixie Machinery and Equipment Company and the record of the latter firm disclosed the Rathford Engineering Company.

In the records this firm was known as a partnership, and each year pains were taken to see that a partnership return of income was filed. The alleged partners reported the share of net income disclosed by this partnership return of income on their respective individual income tax returns and everything went merrily on its way.

The firm came into existence in November 1931. At that time someone discovered that there were some wasteful water leaks in the Kansas City municipal water system. With a great number of men on the payroll of the water department, it would appear to the uninitiated that these water leaks could easily have been detected and repaired by the department's own personnel, but, if such action were taken, how could the loyal adherents of the machine obtain their share of the graft?

The water department did not detect, but it did repair, its water leaks. Instead of doing the detecting, a contract was entered into with the Rathford Engineering Company to pay them $5,000 a month to detect the water leaks. The Kansas City charter had a provision that any contract exceeding $2,500 had to be approved by the city council, but what is a charter between friends? The city council never saw the contract; it was just made.

Delving into the records, the treasury agents discovered that from November 1, 1931, to October 1933, and from December 15, 1934, until November 30, 1938, this firm had operated, receiving $5,000 each month during these periods, or a total of $342,500. Payments had been made twice a month by the city, one warrant being for $3,500, the other for $1,500.

The partnership consisted, as of record, of John J. Rathford, an engineer employed by the city; J. G. Halpin, an attorney of moderate means; and Carl D. Higgins, a construction foreman. They were questioned and, as their stories unfolded, an amazing set of facts was developed. Halpin and Higgins had had nothing whatsoever to do with the Rathford Engineering Company, except that once each year at filing time they would file income tax returns reporting thereon each one-third of the net income of the partnership, an income they never had in their possession. Rathford did act as manager, directed the activities of two or three employees necessary to detect the water leaks, notified the water department where the leaks were so that the department could repair them, and kept a brief set of records. For these services he was paid $325 per month. Each year he also filed an income tax return reporting thereon one-third of the income of the partnership, although he received only the $325 monthly payment.

Special agents Kemp O. Hiatt and Walter E. Rayn and internal revenue agent Louis Herman investigated this case. More and more information was obtained by them until the story was complete. Here is what the agents found:

In 1931, W. D. Boyle and John J. Pryor created this partnership for the purpose of detecting water leaks, but, although they wanted the money, they did not want it known that they were the ones receiving it. So they formed the partnership and told Rathford that he was to be the manager. They also told him he would be considered one of the partners insofar as the records were concerned, and, for the other partners in name only, they called on Halpin who, as an attorney, devoted his time to Boyle's real estate ventures, and Higgins (no relation to Otto—who, as construction foreman, was employed by the Boyle-Pryor Construction Company). A public accountant, C. V. Norfleet, was instructed by Boyle to prepare the partnership returns of income and the individual returns of the three partners for each year.

So the firm started functioning, receiving $60,000 per annum from the city and paying out for labor $10,920. The balance, representing the profits, was paid to Boyle and Pryor, who retained this money, but they did not report it as income. With respect to the payroll, the firm actually needed only one employee, namely a John J. Higinbotham, who received $160 a month and who actually worked, detecting water leaks.[1] Now Rathford was an honest man and, when he was informed that salaries were to be paid to William J. Burnett and Clifton L. Kerr, although Burnett rendered no services whatsoever, he kept his records accordingly. Burnett was a son-in-law of Pendergast and Kerr was a full-time employee of the water department.

Norfleet examined the records of Rathford and found that the latter had recorded the semimonthly payroll as follows:

Name	Total Hours	Monthly Rate	Amount Paid
John J. Rathford	1/2 mo.	$325.00	$162.50
Clifton L. Kerr	1/2 mo.	$125.00	$62.50
John J. Higinbotham	1/2 mo.	$160.00	$80.00
William J. Burnett	1/2 mo.	$300.00	$150.00
Total			$455.00

Norfleet was aghast! What if someone would happen to see that record with Burnett's and Kerr's names thereon? Norfleet ordered Rathford to cease keeping that record and in place thereof furnished Rathford with a corrected form of payroll which would not reflect these names. This form of payroll was as follows:

Name	Total Hours	Monthly Rate	Amount Paid
John J. Rathford	1/2 mo	$375.00	$187.50
Joseph G. Halpin	1/2 mo.	$375.00	$187.50
John J. Higinbotham	1/2 mo.	$160.00	$80.00
Total			$455.00

A simple feat, changing the payroll and still making it agree with the actual amounts paid. No use for Rathford to complain that he had received only $162.50 and that Halpin had not received a penny. Could any of the pseudo partners complain? They had to obey the orders of Boyle or lose their positions and, with the political influences of Boyle and Pryor, could they obtain any other employment in Kansas City?

So as each year passed and the income tax filing period approached, Norfleet would come, examine the records, prepare the partnership returns of income and the individual returns of Rathford, Halpin, and Higgins. He could then require the aforementioned three to sign their respective individual income tax returns, without consulting with them about the contents of the returns, or allowing them to examine the returns, and they were not required to swear to the correctness of the returns. In fact, they gave Norfleet no information whatsoever with respect to income or deductions and they never knew what had actually been reported. Norfleet prepared the returns solely from the information he obtained personally and, after requiring them to sign the returns, he took the returns away with him. Neither Rathford, Halpin, nor Higgins ever paid a cent of the taxes disclosed by the returns. Possibly Boyle or Pryor or both paid these taxes, since the income these men were reporting actually belonged to those two persons and they profited by having three exemptions reduce the income and by avoiding the payment of higher surtax rates.

On at least one occasion Norfleet did not bother to have Halpin even sign the return he had prepared for him; instead he signed Halpin's name to the return. Norfleet admitted, when questioned about this signature, that he had signed the name of Halpin to the return, but stated he had done so because the latter was absent from the city at that time.

Now Norfleet was a public accountant with many years' experience and practice and he knew full well that, if he signed a return as agent for another, he would sign his own name with a notation that he was acting as agent.

Another interesting angle appeared with respect to the year 1938. Boyle died in June of that year and, after the close of the year, Norfleet began to prepare the returns. Rathford, Halpin, and Higgins objected to signing them. They felt that they were only under obligation to Boyle to sign the returns. They told Norfleet that, since they had not received the income and since Boyle was now dead, they were under no obligations to continue the practice followed in the other years. Rathford, Halpin, and Higgins were honest men who did not relish the deceptions practiced, but, since they had to have employment and since Boyle, their boss, could, by his political influence, keep employment from them, they were forced under the circumstances to agree to practice the deceptions. So as soon as Boyle was dead and their obligations to him were no longer in effect, they rebelled against further wrongdoing.

Norfleet told them that the Rathford Engineering Company was winding up its business and that these returns were the last ones that they would be required to file. He further told them that they had better sign these last returns or else the government would investigate why no returns had been filed and that perhaps the entire scheme in the prior years would be brought to light.

Rathford, Halpin, and Higgins were willing witnesses and aided the treasury agents in determining the true state of affairs. Their testimony that the income of the firm actually belonged to Boyle and Pryor was valuable in determining some of the income these two persons had received. In addition, these three were not men of wealth and they and their families were dependent upon their salaries, so they could not afford to risk the displeasure of Boyle and Pryor who, with their influence, could keep them from earning a living. So, although they were technically guilty of conspiring to aid in the evasion of income taxes of Boyle and Pryor by reporting on returns, signed by them, income not their own, but belonging to those two persons, it was decided that no action should be taken against them. To this, U.S. Attorney Milligan agreed.

With respect to Norfleet, however, a different situation existed. He was widely conversant with the income tax laws and he had been entrusted with an enrollment to practice as an accountant before the Treasury Department, in connection with his enrollment, having sworn to uphold the income tax laws and regulations. Therefore, his flagrant disregard of the income tax laws and regulations was all the more reprehensible.

Accordingly, Milligan presented the facts to the grand jury, and on January 11, 1940, Norfleet was indicted on nine counts, charging him with willfully aiding, assisting in, counseling, procuring, and advising the preparation and presentation of false income tax returns. He was arrested on January 12, 1940, and released on $3,500 bond pending his arraignment on January 22, 1940. When arraigned he pleaded not guilty, and his trial was set for February 6,

1940. The case was continued until April 29, 1940, due to one of Norfleet's attorneys withdrawing from the case.

When the case was called again on April 29, 1940, before Federal Judge Collet, Norfleet pleaded guilty to the first two counts, assistant U.S. Attorney Richard K. Phelps agreeing to the dismissal of the seven other counts in the indictment. He was sentenced to serve six months in jail on count one and two years in the penitentiary on count two, the sentence on count two being suspended and the defendant placed on probation for two years to begin after he had served his time on the first count.

On May 16, 1940, Higgins was found unconscious in an alley behind a taproom, suffering from a skull fracture which witnesses said he suffered when he fell and struck his head against the pavement. His clothing was disheveled and his right coat pocket was ripped. He was taken to police headquarters, but, when he failed to regain consciousness, he was removed to a hospital. He died on May 19, 1940.[2]

Nineteen

Matthew S. Murray

A S STATED IN CHAPTER 17, an investigation of the income tax liability of Pryor disclosed that certain government bonds purchased by him had found their way into the possession of Matthew S. Murray. This was interesting information.

Murray, a civil engineer, born at Dayton, Ohio, fifty-six years of age, had been appointed May 1, 1926, to the position of director of public works of Kansas City. This appointment was made by McElroy, the city manager, at the request of Pendergast. It can readily be seen why Pendergast wanted Murray, a close friend of his, as director of public works. This position entailed the granting of contract and noncontract jobs on public works to contractors, and Pendergast was the chief stockholder in the Ready Mixed Concrete Company, the Midwest Paving Company, and the Mid-West Pre Cote Company. His friend could make it possible that these Pendergast corporations would not be slighted when contracts were let.

Pryor, a chief stockholder of the Dixie Machinery and Equipment Company, the Boyle-Pryor Construction Company, and the Missouri Asphalt Products Company, also was in favor of Murray obtaining that position.

Under the city charter, work for less than $2,500 could be given to contractors without calling for bids and also without the approval of the city council. Naturally, Murray would favor the Pendergast and Pryor organizations in such instances, and it also was not difficult to break a large job exceeding $2,500 into sufficient smaller projects under $2,500 to avoid the embarrassment of having some outsider underbid these organizations. So Murray got the job at $9,000 per annum.

On June 1, 1935, he received a federal appointment as state administrator for Missouri for the Works Progress Administration at $6,500 per annum. Now he had a greater field in which to operate and to let contracts for work not confined to Kansas City alone. Pendergast and Pryor did not feel disappointed. Their friend was in a still better position to help them get good contracts. But they still wanted him to keep his Kansas City job, so, until October 21, 1939, when he resigned his federal position, he acted in a dual capacity, taking care of his federal position during most of each week and his city position during the weekends.

It would not be expected that Pendergast and Pryor would leave any favors Murray gave them go unrewarded.

Special agents E. A. Hayes and A. W. Fleming and internal revenue agent A. R. Baker were assigned to investigate the income tax liability of Murray. His salary from his city position was exempt from federal taxation, but his federal salary was not, so he filed income tax returns each year reporting that salary, but, since he was married and had three children, the taxes paid were very nominal.

The treasury agents soon discovered that Murray was using currency for expenses and investments greatly in excess of the two salaries he was receiving, and they were puzzled at first as to the source of this excess currency.

It was found that he deposited large sums of currency in a brokerage account which was carried in the name of "Robert E. King," that he deposited large sums of currency in his bank accounts, and that he purchased stocks and real estate with currency. In addition, he paid expenses with currency, bought his wife a fur coat, paying for it with currency and, after an exhaustive search, the treasury agents had Murray using for investments and disbursements from 1929 to 1938, inclusive, $226,224.41, when his salaries for this period amounted to only $106,750. This meant that Murray had received approximately $120,000 from some source other than his salaries.

Questioned about the use of so much excess money, Murray finally admitted that Pryor had given him bonds, currency, a diamond ring, and had paid the tuition of one of Murray's sons at an eastern school preparatory to the son's entering West Point Military Academy. He also admitted that he had received money from Schneider and that on one occasion he had been given an interest in a firm which handled a construction contract, a contract which he had, as state administrator of the Works Progress Administration, given to that firm. His contention was that he had considered all of this as gifts, or gratuities, and that for that reason they had not been reported by him as income.

The treasury agents had previously discovered that in 1935 the Boyle-Pryor Construction Company and Thomas L. Farrington of St. Louis secured a contract for the rehabilitation of the Missouri state prison, Jefferson City, which was a Public Works Administration grant. Farrington stated that when the contract had been secured, Pryor in speaking of Murray had told him that Murray was to get a 25 percent interest in the profits realized from the contract, saying, "We have got to cut the old chief [Murray] in on this contract. He has done a lot for us and we are under great obligations to him." Farrington said that Murray received the 25 percent share of the proceeds of the profit realized on this project, which amounted to approximately $30,000.

Murray considered the money given him as gifts. When a gift is based upon a consideration for services rendered, it loses its designation as a gift, at least insofar as income taxes are concerned. Pendergast and Pryor certainly did not give this money to Murray because they loved him or had any great affection for him. It must have been paid to him for some services he had rendered to them. So the treasury agents began an investigation to determine whether such services had been rendered.

It was found that in 1933, Murray had recommended to the Missouri highway commission that the Boyle-Pryor Construction Company be given the contract for resurfacing projects on Highways 37 and 71 in Barry and McDonald Counties. Although the minutes of the commission disclosed the purported awarding of the contract to the Boyle-Pryor Construction Company, the same was not executed by the commission because of an opinion of the general counsel, who held it to be illegal for the reason that it had not been advertised and because of excessive mileage awarded to one contractor. By that time the work was practically completed and the contractor had received about 75 percent of the consideration named in the contract. Actuated partly because of public indignation over the manner in which this work was handled, and in particular the excessive cost and inferior character thereof, the commission, some members of which did not even know that a contract had been awarded or that work had been begun and the project practically completed, withheld further payments until

March 1935, when a compromise settlement was made whereby the contractors accepted about $40,000 less than provided by the contract, which never was executed by the commission. The Boyle-Pryor Construction Company allegedly realized excessive profit from this project, and while it was not established that any portion thereof was paid to Murray, yet it was brought out that he unduly interested himself on behalf of these contractors in securing employment in a highly irregular manner, with the result that a public scandal threatened, and that he was seen with the contractors on the site of the work.

An investigation of the city records disclosed that during the period 1932 to 1938 the Pryor group of firms was allotted awards totaling $2,311,829.29 and the Pendergast firms $1,482,001.57. These figures include only the noncontract transactions, consisting of items of $2,500 or under on which no bids were asked. In order to break up the contracts in such small amounts, over 3,341 purchase vouchers, less than $2,500, had to be issued, and an examination disclosed that often several invoices and purchase orders bore the same date, covered the same type of material or service, but the amount of each was slightly under $2,500 to evade the requirements of the city charter.

The records of the state disclosed that WPA contracts were awarded the Pryor-Pendergast firms in an amount of $1,151,935.32. An interesting angle in connection with these awards is that the Ready Mixed Concrete Company, owned by Pendergast, received $993,281.25 of these awards. In General Order No. 120, dated April 15, 1937, the assistant administrator of the national WPA referred to use of ready mixed concrete on projects and stated, in part: "There are many jobs, however, such as paving of airport runways, where concrete can and should be mixed at the site of the work and where a substantial amount of labor can thus be used without materially adding to the unit cost of the work."

Subsequent to that order the Kansas City municipal airport was rebuilt and modernized in a joint city and WPA project, both controlled by Murray. The project included the rebuilding of runways. The concrete was furnished by the Ready Mixed Concrete Company, plant-mixed, and to justify the purchase of plant-mixed concrete, a statement was included in the contracts reading, "Operating conditions are such as to preclude mixing the concrete at the site of the work." Photographs taken at the site during the progress of the construction disclosed that conditions were not such as to preclude the mixing of concrete at the site.

Information was also obtained that contracts specifying plant-mixed concrete in the Kansas City area were twice those specifying similar material in the St. Louis area, which is twice as large as Kansas City. Testimony was also obtained that the Ready Mixed Concrete Company was the only available source of such material in the Kansas City area.

There was no question but that Pendergast and Pryor were favored in every way possible when it came to the awarding of contracts, and it can be readily understood why Murray received such, as he termed them, "gifts and gratuities."

U.S. Attorney Milligan presented the evidence to the grand jury and on October 26, 1939, Murray was indicted on five counts charging evasion of income taxes for the years 1934 to 1938 in an amount of $6,577.28.

The case came to trial at Kansas City on March 4, 1940, before U.S. Judge Albert L. Reeves, who by stipulation sat as a jury, and on March 13, 1940, after hearing the evidence, the court rendered a verdict of guilty. On March 18, 1940, Judge Reeves in passing sentence said:

> It was my sincere hope that the unpleasant duty of this hour might have been avoided. The deprivation of liberty or property of any person by the sentence of the law is ever a hard and heavy task for the judge imposing such sentence. It is especially painful in this case. The defendant has borne a well merited, good reputation. His friends are many and devoted. He has enjoyed an unusually high degree of success. His thorough education, supplemented by natural endowments made him very useful as a civil engineer. His services were in demand and his future seemed secure.
>
> His usefulness is at least temporarily ended for the causes all too plainly revealed in the evidence. Men with sinister and selfish purposes gradually undermined the bulwarks and palladia of a good life and character and finally the crash came. The defendant permitted himself to be drawn into an atmosphere and an environment of low standards. He harkened to the voice of the tempter and forsook the people it was his duty faithfully to serve. He has given up so much for paltry and passing material gain.
>
> In the foreground of this case is his offense in attempting to evade his income tax but in the background is the serious

moral delinquency in debauching his high and responsible offices for the sordid income, the tax upon which he sought to
evade.

The punishment should be and will be in harmony with
sentences imposed in other similar cases in this district.

Let it now be the judgment and sentence of the law that the
defendant be committed to the custody of the Attorney General of the United States for a period of two years to be confined in some penal institution of the type of that at
Leavenworth, Kansas, on the first count, and with the same
sentence on each of the other four counts. It is ordered, however, that the sentences on the second, third, fourth and fifth
counts be made to run concurrently with each other and each
to run concurrently with the sentence on the first count so that
the maximum period of the defendant's imprisonment will be
two years. The usual custom will be followed by omitting
costs.

An appeal was filed with the Eighth U.S. Circuit Court of Appeals which on January 31, 1941, affirmed the sentence imposed by
the district court. On March 20, 1941, Murray entered Leavenworth
Penitentiary.

The opinion of the circuit court of appeals, in part, stated:

The only evidence in the record inconsistent with the defendant's guilt is his testimony that he received gifts. The lower
court, whose business it was to judge the credibility of the witnesses, held that this testimony was incredible.

His secretive use of cash, his explanation of his right to the
"cut" in the prison contract and his favoritism to the concern in
which the donors had an interest, are all inconsistent with the
innocent receipt of gifts.[1]

Twenty

The Grand Jury, the United States Attorney

O N JANUARY 13, 1939, a federal grand jury was im-
paneled in the western district of Missouri by U.S. District
Judge Albert L. Reeves. In his charge to the grand jury,
Judge Reeves concluded by saying:

> Gentlemen, you have a great task. I have gone into this matter
> for the reason that it might be suggested that you needed con-
> crete illustrations of what is going on in Kansas City in order to
> justify the inquiry that you gentlemen are called upon to make.
> I charge you gentlemen to begin the siege of the citadel of orga-
> nized, licensed and protected crime in Kansas City and that
> you will not lift the siege until either you or your successors
> have broken down the walls and the fortifications of an orga-
> nized, licensed and protected crime, until you have brought
> these men before the bar of justice. Gentlemen, that is the re-
> sponsibility that rests upon you. Every citizen ought to be
> eager and anxious for his country's welfare, to move upon a
> situation that is as startling as the one that I have given you
> today. Gentlemen, you have a great responsibility.

Prior to this concluding statement Judge Reeves had told the
grand jury that there were literally hundreds of gambling clubs operating in Kansas City and that these clubs were paying tribute to a
certain "big man." Judge Reeves suggested that the grand jury attempt to break down this racket and called attention to the fact that
the income tax laws had been used to great advantage in other
places in breaking up racketeering.

It was obvious that Judge Reeves had in mind Carrollo when he
referred to the big man, but no one would have believed, even with

the most vivid imagination, that before this grand jury was discharged even a mightier man than Carrollo would fall.

At the time the grand jury began to function, the treasury agents had already made important discoveries. They had found that a payoff in the fire insurance rate litigation settlement had been made; they had traced the payoff fund to Street in Chicago and then some of it from him to McCormack in St. Louis; they had found documentary proof that meetings had been held between Street, O'Malley the state insurance superintendent, and McCormack; and that Pendergast in Kansas City had been interested in the settlement, and they had evidence that McCormack had not retained all of the payoff fund traced to him. Furthermore, they had delved deep into the financial affairs of Pendergast and had found that Pendergast annually used currency in excess of a half million dollars over what he reported annually as income.

U.S. Attorney Milligan by now had proven that he was a fearless and competent prosecutor. He had for the past two years prosecuted hundreds of vote fraud cases, which was in direct defiance of the Pendergast machine. What annoyed Milligan was the fact that in these vote fraud prosecutions he was not getting the big men, the ones who were directing and ordering the commission of crime, instead of the little precinct judges and clerks who were being convicted and sent to prison, too afraid for their lives and the lives of their loved ones to tell who had ordered them to make elections a farce.[1]

Both federal judges Otis and Reeves had also shown that they did not fear the machine or its adherents. Time after time charges were given by them to grand juries "to get the big men," and now Judge Reeves had again made a similar charge to this new grand jury.[2]

Led by Max Schrier of Savannah, Missouri, as foreman, and Ray Moore of Chillicothe, secretary, the grand jury enthusiastically entered in on its duties. It was a fearless group of men, but where should they start? Even if witnesses called before them would testify that they had paid tribute to someone, no federal law would have been violated. Only if it could be proven that this tribute had not been reported by the recipient on his income tax return would a federal statute be available for use.

Of necessity, evidence to prove an income tax law violation is not so simple to develop and it takes investigators, trained in the tax laws, with all of the ramifications and experience in tracing transactions through a maze of intricate avenues to delve into the financial affairs of taxpayers. The treasury agents of the Intelligence Unit were doing that very thing.

Case after case was presented to the grand jury until finally on October 27, 1939, after nine months of service, a final report was submitted to Judge Reeves and the grand jury was discharged. It had done its work well and, as a result, the big men of Kansas City were either in prison or awaiting trial.

Pendergast, O'Malley, Carrollo, Higgins, Pryor, Murray, every one a powerful leader once, now only a convict or an ex-convict.

As the leaders of the machine toppled and fell, other violations of the law also were brought into view. Treasury agents of the Bureau of Narcotics had for some time been conducting a secret investigation, as a result of which the grand jury on April 19, 1939, returned twenty-three true bills, naming twelve men, for violation of the narcotics laws. It had been discovered that Kansas City was the distribution point for heroin sales estimated at $1 million a month.

Twenty-One

Conclusion

As in all such large income tax cases, there were numerous smaller collateral cases developed which were of a minor character and on which only the tax and penalties were collected. Some of these are included in the following statistics, disclosing the results of the Kansas City income tax investigations commenced in May 1938 and completed in March 1940.

Number of special agents participating	10
Number of internal revenue agents participating	16
Number of individuals and corporations investigated	22
Number of tax years investigated	121
Aggregate amount of additional income found	$8,237,915.14
Aggregate amount of income taxes recommended for assessment	$3,175,258.14
Aggregate amount of penalties proposed for assessment	$985,340.16
Number of indictments returned (income tax)	9
Number of indictments returned (perjury)	2
Number of total counts in indictments (income tax)	40
Number of total counts in indictments (perjury)	2
Number of convictions after trial	2
Number of indictments dismissed (Jordan purged himself of the perjury charge by appearing before the grand jury and testifying)	1
Total number of years defendants were sentenced to serve	19-7/12
Total number of years defendants were placed on probation	20
Total amount of fines assessed	$37,500.00

Much had transpired between May 9, 1938, when three treasury agents were called to Washington and assigned to investigate the then alleged payoff in the settlement of the fire insurance rate litigation in Missouri, and March 18, 1940, when the last "big shot" of the Kansas City machine, Matthew Murray, was found guilty of income tax evasion.

Men considered immune from prosecution had seen the iron gates of Leavenworth Penitentiary close behind them, and the citizens of Kansas City held in bondage for many years were again able to enjoy the rights granted them by the Constitution. Pendergast, the leader, under whose domination gambling, prostitution, and racketeering flourished, merchants paid tribute in order to be allowed the privilege of conducting their business, ballot boxes were stuffed making it impossible for any person who would not subscribe to the machine policies to be elected to office, was gone.[1]

So also had gone Carrollo, who collected tribute from the merchants and who used the machine gun and the bomb on anyone who dared to oppose him; Higgins, the director of police, whose department protected all citizens loyal to Pendergast and the machine, condoning the prevalent vices as long as those participating therein remained loyal and paid tribute, but offered no protection to those citizens who had the temerity to oppose the machine; and McElroy, the city manager, who ran the city for the benefit of Pendergast and his faction, answering the complaints of decent citizens with wisecracks.

What conditions had existed are perhaps best summed up in the final report of the federal grand jury, which states, in part:

> Conditions were brought to light, which when thoroughly investigated proved the old axiom that "Truth is stranger than fiction." Not only gambling, but vice and racketeering of every conceivable kind and type were being carried on under the protection of the machine. This political machine, controlled with an iron hand by T. J. Pendergast, completely dominated city and county government. . . .
>
> We were faced with the realization that local law enforcement agencies of Kansas City and Jackson County were hopelessly mired in machine politics and state law was unable to afford any protection to its citizens relative to the conditions under which they were forced to work and live. . . .
>
> Continued investigation brought to light the domination of the city government and how the local taxpayers were being

used to finance and perpetuate the machine in power. Even the police force of the city was in the hands of the machine and dominated by one of the lieutenants. Police protection and power was used to enforce many of the machine demands upon individual citizens. It was revealed that a condition had grown up where individuals, and business firms as well, were ruled by fear. They were afraid to oppose the machine for fear of being run out of business, closed up, intimidated in various ways, and even afraid of their lives.

Details of the rottenness of conditions and the power wielded by the machine and Pendergast as its head have received wide publicity since the lengthy investigation of them by this jury. There is no need for us to go into any greater detail relative to this lawlessness. It is inconceivable to the average law-abiding citizen that such a condition could and would be permitted to grow up under our democratic form of government. It is a travesty on justice that criminal laws of every nature can be violated and the violators wield so much influence over law enforcement that it is ultimately necessary for the federal government to step in and break up such a situation by means of the income tax law. . . .

We are glad to have the privilege of serving this court and the people of this district and trust that the service rendered will be of some lasting value in returning law and order to its rightful position. One reward will be seeing Kansas City and the State of Missouri continue its advancement and maintain the position it is rightfully entitled to in these United States. We trust this report of our conduct during our nine months' term will meet with the approval of this court, and ask your honor to finally discharge our body.

Respectfully submitted

Max B. Schrier,
Foreman

Attest:
   Ray Moore,
   Secretary

Thus spoke the grand jury and thus closed the investigation of the Kansas City cases.

A final summation of the work performed is contained in an anonymous poem which was printed in the *Kansas City Star* as of March 24, 1940:

The gravy train was loaded and was heading down the track.
Pendergast was engineer, Pryor rode the back,

Carrollo shoveled in the coal, Higgins hustled freight,
Matt Murray trailed along behind, some twenty minutes late.

The way was clear, the switches set, the whistle gave a hoot
And down the line they balled the jack with fifty feet of loot.
The drivers spun, the engine shook and round the curve she
    veered,
While half the people trembled and half the people cheered.

They whistled loudly at each bend, the semaphores they
    cleared,
With Chief Reed's fingerprint machine the only thing they
    feared.[2]
While all the bosses rode in state and made a mighty show
Ten thousand politicians hung upon the rods below.

The first car held the payroll sack and that was easy dough.
The crew would grab a part of each and no one needs to know.
The second held the paving jobs, the third the building bids,
All rightly sealed, and Pryor's gang was sitting on the lid.

And there were cars for water leaks, and grafts both large and
    small.
The garbage car, a juicy one, they rated best of all.
One palace car, the boss's own, was trimmed in solid gold
And held the risk case settlement of which he never told.

But suddenly a crash occurred, and then the smashup came.
The engineer perhaps was wrong, at least he got the blame.
His mighty train was in the ditch, he couldn't put it back,
For in a careless moment, he had swiped the railroad track.

Appendix

National Fire Insurance Companies Doing Business in Missouri

The State of Missouri brought suit against the companies and fined them on the basis of their impounded premiums as of May 1, 1935. Charles R. Street had required contributions of 5 percent. Missouri's fines were approximately four times Street's assessments, except that for companies giving Street less than $2,500 the minimum fine was $10,000. Sources: District Court, Western District of Missouri Central Divison, Equity, no. 270, *Transcript of Testimony*, I; *Missouri Reports* 355 (March 1947): 1133-36.

	Impounded Premiums	Fines
Aetna Ins. Co.	$216,548.93	$43,000
Agricultural Ins. Co.	40,817.91	10,000
Alliance Ins. Co. of Philadelphia	21,548.61	10,000
American Alliance Ins. Co.	79,881.29	16,000
American Central Ins. Co.	151,771.51	30,000
American Eagle Fire Ins. Co.	47,205.52	10,000
American Ins. Co.	$177,898.21	36,000
American Union Ins. Co.	25,148.39	10,000
Atlas Ins. Co., Ltd.	43,183.47	10,000
Automobile Ins. Co.	106,358.42	21,000
Bankers & Shippers Ins. Co.	41,219.47	10,000
Boston Ins. Co.	105,011.03	21,000
British American Assur. Co.	10,843.79	10,000
Caledonian Ins. Co.	9,910.15	10,000

California Ins. Co.	19,563.29	10,000
Camden Fire Ins. Assoc.	46,031.80	10,000
Central States Fire Ins. Co.	33,593.90	10,000
Chicago Fire & Marine Ins. Co.	10,343.90	
Citizens Ins. Co.	55,243.91	11,000
City of New York Ins. Co.	53,424.03	11,000
Columbia Fire Ins. Co.	16,482.40	10,000
Columbia Ins. Co. of New Jersey	3,801.89	10,000
Commerce Ins. Co.	7,730.55	10,000
Commercial Union Assur. Co., Ltd.	67,864.87	14,000
Commercial Union Fire Ins. Co.	27,693.88	10,000
Concordia Fire Ins. Co. of Milwaukee	57,164.80	12,000
Connecticut Fire Ins. Co.	100,235.62	20,000
Continental Ins. Co.	286,528.44	54,000
County Fire Ins. Co. of Philadelphia	5,190.77	10,000
Detroit Fire & Marine	17,948.57	
Dubuque Fire & Marine	58,190.05	12,000
Eagle Fire Co. of N.Y.	17,931.97	10,000
Eagle Star & Brit. Dom. Ins. Co.	20,571.54	10,000
East & West Ins. Co.	26,051.21	10,000
Equitable Fire & Marine Ins. Co.	35,721.19	10,000
Federal Union Ins. Co.	12,876.29	10,000
Fidelity-Phoenix Fire Ins. Co.	336,691.80	68,000
Fire Ass'n of Philadelphia	77,097.25	15,000
Fireman's Fund Ins. Co.	114,784.23	23,000
Fireman's Ins. Co.	120,247.98	25,000
First American Fire Ins. Co.	26,070.88	10,000
Franklin Fire Ins. Co. of Phila.	161,292.23	32,000
Franklin National Ins. Co.	18,967.58	10,000
Girard Fire & Marine Ins. Co.	36,404.96	10,000
Glen Falls Ins. Co.	49,817.05	10,000
Globe & Rutgers Fire Ins. Co.	57,056.22	11,000
Granite State Fire Ins. Co.	16,359.30	10,000
Great American Ins. Co.	219,232.70	44,000
Guaranty Fire Ins. Co.	5,806.88	
Hanover Fire Ins. Co.	82,329.66	16,000
Hartford Fire Ins. Co.	476,581.87	94,000
Home Fire & Marine Ins. Co.	25,184.57	10,000
Home Ins. Co.	658,926.75	132,000
Hudson Ins. Co.	12,313.37	

Imperial Assur. Co.	21,270.09	10,000
Importers & Exporters	49,645.05	
Ins. Co. of North America	178,067.72	36,000
Ins. Co. of State of Pa.	37,533.74	10,000
Law, Union & Rock Ins. Co., Ltd.	26,152.68	10,000
Liverpool, London & Globe Ins. Co., Ltd.	172,944.26	35,000
London Assur. Corp.	59,945.48	12,000
London & Lancashire Ins. Co., Ltd.	75,051.09	15,000
London & Provincial Marine & General Ins. Co., Ltd	9,653.79	10,000
London & Scottish Assur. Corp., Ltd.	13,466.59	10,000
Lumberman's Ins. Co.	32,135.01	10,000
Manhattan Fire & Marine Ins. Co.	9,933.90	10,000
Massachusetts Fire & Marine Ins. Co.	15,635.29	10,000
Mechanics & Traders Ins. Co.	32,897.51	10,000
Mechanics Ins. Co.	7,743.24	
Merchants Fire Assur. Corp. of N.Y.	60,259.86	12,000
Merchants Fire Ins. Co.	12,138.27	10,000
Merchants Ins. Co. of Providence	20,218.04	10,000
Mercury Ins. Co.	26,607.44	10,000
Michigan Fire & Marine Ins. Co.	15,834.79	10,000
Milwaukee Mechanics Ins. Co.	67,754.50	14,000
Minneapolis Fire & Marine Ins. Co.	22,571.18	
National Ben Franklin Fire Ins. Co.	27,198.68	10,000
National Fire Ins. Co. of Hartford	307,912.43	61,000
National Liberty Ins. Co. of America	85,207.70	17,000
National Reserve Ins. Co.	13,521.30	10,000
National Security Fire Ins. Co.	11,043.86	10,000
National Union Fire Ins. Co.	80,379.93	16,000
Newark Fire Ins. Co.	28,521.63	10,000
New England Fire Ins. Co.	15,949.12	10,000
New Hampshire Fire Ins. Co.	76,684.24	15,000
New Jersey Ins. Co.	28,045.44	
N.Y. Underwriters Ins. Co.	150,931.36	30,000
Niagara Fire Ins. Co.	49,965.79	10,000
Northern Assur. Co., Ltd.	84,743.20	13,000
Northern Ins. Co. of New York	72,784.14	17,000
North River Ins. Co.	67,320.42	14,000
Northwestern Fire & Marine Ins. Co.	13,107.78	10,000

Norwich Union Fire Ins. Society, Ltd.	44,027.49	10,000
Old Colony Ins. Co.	16,932.00	10,000
Orient Ins. Co.	70,124.78	14,000
Pacific Fire Ins. Co.	32,043.43	10,000
Palatine Ins. Co., Ltd.	33,383.92	10,000
Patriotic Ins. Co. of America	4,986.23	10,000
Philadelphia Fire & Marine Ins. Co.	51,064.11	10,000
Phoenix Assur. Co., Ltd. of London	77,303.92	15,000
Phoenix Ins. Co.	120,532.85	24,000
Pittsburgh Underwriters	2,998.69	
Potomac Ins. Co. of D.C.	49,014.84	
Presidential Fire & Marine Ins. Co.	3,546.55	
Providence Washington Ins. Co.	43,734.55	10,000
Provident Fire Ins. Co.	7,703.65	10,000
Queen Ins. Co. of America	102,937.62	21,000
Reliance Ins. Co. of Philadelphia	20,913.67	10,000
Rhode Island Ins. Co.	52,961.55	12,000
Royal Exchange Assur.	109,699.40	22,000
Royal Ins. Co., Ltd.	97,997.48	20,000
Safeguard Ins. Co.	9,907.90	10,000
St. Paul Fire & Marine Ins. Co.	82,435.64	16,000
Scottish Union & National Ins. Co.	88,290.17	18,000
Security Ins. Co. of New Haven	59,215.01	12,000
Sentinel Fire Ins. Co.	20,644.32	10,000
Springfield Fire & Marine Ins. Co.	264,002.48	53,000
Standard Fire Ins. Co. of Conn.	26,811.21	10,000
Standard Fire Ins. Co. of N.J.	57,820.53	12,000
Star Ins. Co. of America	28,730.90	10,000
State Assur. Co.	10,303.33	
Stuyvesant Ins. Co.	23,428.35	
Sun Ins. Office Ltd.	71,821.20	14,000
Superior Fire Ins. Co.	20,304.31	
Swan Fire & Life Ins. Co.	12,958.26	
Tokio Marine & Fire Ins. Co.	35,957.32	
Transcontinental Ins. Co.	13,324.72	10,000
Travelers Fire Ins. Co.	174,764.18	35,000
Twin City Fire Ins. Co.	9,855.00	10,000
Underwriters Grain Association	41,419.67	
Union Assur. Society Ltd.	15,356.05	10,000

Union Fire Ins. Co.	15,872.72	10,000
United Firemen's Ins. Co. of Phila.	2,147.70	10,000
United States Fire Ins. Co.	151,984.68	30,000
U.S. Merchants & Shippers	8,379.96	
Victory Ins. Co.	12,622.45	
Westchester Fire Ins. Co.	71,348.10	14,000
Western Assur. Co.	18,511.32	10,000
Western Fire Ins. Co.	33,932.74	
World Fire and Marine Ins. Co.	23,290.23	10,000
Yorkshire Ins. Co., Ltd.	39,458.64	10,000
	$9,020,279.01	$2,080,000

Notes

Chapter One

1. Little is known of Pendergast's early years. His attendance at the above-mentioned high school is uncertain, and records of two similarly named colleges in Kansas, one at St. Marys, the other at Leavenworth, do not list his name. See Lawrence H. Larsen and Nancy J. Hulston, *Pendergast!* 22. He does appear to have played sandlot baseball.

2. James Francis Pendergast, known as Alderman Jim, left St. Joseph in 1876, and after working in a Kansas City meat plant and then an iron foundry, entered the tavern business in the city's industrial and slum area, the West Bottoms, in the early 1880s, purchasing the American House in 1881—a two-story combination saloon, boardinghouse, and hotel. In 1887 he became Democratic committeeman for the first ward. He represented his ward on the city council until 1910, when he resigned. He had contracted Bright's disease, and died the next year. Ibid., 15–21.

3. Pendergast always gave the year of his marriage as 1907. The bride was the former Carolyn Elizabeth Dunn Snider. There may have been two ceremonies, civil in 1907, Roman Catholic in 1911. Ibid., 41. The city's premier real estate developer, J. C. Nichols, in the mid-1920s constructed one of the first shopping malls in the United States some blocks to the south of central Kansas City, next to the city's most fashionable avenue, Ward Parkway, which was Nichols's development too. A French Regency mansion, the Pendergast house boasted a spacious hall, wrought-iron stairs, and paneled walls. "The combination of rose-hued bricks, laid in white mortar, with soft-shaded slate, makes the few exterior decorations stand out prominently. The massive wrought-iron door with its vertical panes of glass, the cut stone cornucopia placed above the stone frame that encloses it, and three sturdy chimneys attract the eye of the beholder." So it was described in the *Kansas City Star*. Robert H. Ferrell, *Harry S. Truman: A Life*, 95. Estimates of its cost varied, from $125,000 to $150,000 and more. This in an era when an ordinary house might cost $4,000 or $5,000.

4. Gnefkow was essentially a clerk within the boss's office, and never

was implicated in anything illegal. Despite having no law degree, he became a city magistrate in 1947, and served on the bench for thirty years.

5. For the efforts of common citizens to oppose the machine, see the
Larsen and Hulston book mentioned above and William M. Reddig, *Tom's
Town: Kansas City and the Pendergast Legend.* The first serious effort to deal
with the machine was led by Rabbi Samuel S. Mayerberg in 1932, whose
Chronicle of an American Crusader, mostly a memoir of his religious life as
rabbi eventually of the influential Kansas City temple, B'nai Jehudah, contains a final chapter relating his reform activities in 1932. He managed to
galvanize the local ministerial association, but after a few months his
movement petered out, failing of lack of financial support and local indif-
ference. The more important National Youth Movement, a group of young
businessmen, lawyers, and college students, entered the municipal elections of 1934, but again failed, after an orgy of violence in which four people
were killed by machine goons and dozens more were hospitalized or
beaten up.

6. It is unclear whether Pendergast could control Lazia, and the pre-
sumption might well be that he could not, that the gangster was able to
exert great pressure on the machine's leader who could not easily disown
his actions.

7. An interpretation by the state supreme court made horse racing possible, as a game in which an individual could make a contribution for im-
provement of a horse's breed. A test was necessary. If the animal whose
breeding was being assisted by the contribution happened to run, perhaps
minutes later, in competition against other horses, on an oval track with
lines at the start and finish, and ran first, the investor in the horse's breed
became eligible for a "refund." The racetracks had windows labeled "Contributions" and "Refunds." Judge Park's connection with horse racing in
Platte County is unclear; there may have been none. When Pendergast first
heard Park's name mentioned as a candidate for governor, he supposedly
said, "Who the hell is Park?"

Chapter Two

1. In Missouri's two principal cities, St. Louis and Kansas City, many
immigrants did not take out citizenship papers. Others did, and were
Italian-Americans, to employ the hyphenated term popularized by former
president Theodore Roosevelt in World War I.

2. The description is confusing. The Intelligence Unit was in the Bureau
of Internal Revenue, Department of the Treasury, and so of course were the
agents with offices in major cities across the country.

3. For many years Kansas City's police department was under control
of the governor of Missouri, but in 1932 the city manager, McElroy, chal-
lenged this control, in favor of "home rule." The change from state to local
control was hailed as an advance of good government. In 1939, after the
fall of the Pendergast machine, the Missouri legislature placed the Kansas

City police department back under state control. During the 1930s it was discovered that one out of ten of the department's officers possessed police records.

4. Clay County lies directly north of Kansas City and Jackson County, and the names testify to their historical beginnings. The county seat of Jackson County was (until establishment of a second courthouse in Kansas City) Independence; the seat of Clay County is Liberty.

5. Lazia's income was enormous, considering average income in the 1920s. The decade marked the high point of employee and worker income during the first thirty years of the century. Clerks in manufacturing averaged $2,426 per year in 1926; postal workers, $2,128; federal government employees in executive departments, $1,809; anthracite coal miners, $1,691; iron and steel workers, $1,687; railway clerks, $1,604; teachers, $1,277; telephone employees, $1,117. Farmers' incomes, difficult to measure because farmers were somewhat self-sufficient, were considerably less. Admittedly, income taxes for such incomes were slight or nonexistent.

6. For failure to file a proper income tax return the statute of limitations was three years. Lazia's filing date for 1929 would be March 15, 1930. (In those years the filing date was March 15, not April 15.)

7. The senior Walsh had practiced in Kansas City until the World War, when President Woodrow Wilson appointed him co-chairman of the National Labor Board, of which the other co-chairman was former president William H. Taft. After the war Walsh established law offices in New York and Washington and did not return to Kansas City, leaving his younger partner, James P. Aylward, in charge, together with Walsh's son Jerome. Aylward was chairman of the Jackson County Democratic Committee and, beginning in 1923, the party's state chairman.

8. Milligan's brother Jacob was a longtime member of the U.S. House of Representatives from Richmond, north of Kansas City.

9. A supersedeas bond ensured a stay of proceedings, pending appeal.

10. As the end approached, Lazia supposedly said, "If anything happens, notify Tom Pendergast, my best friend, and tell him I love him." The funeral was the largest in the city's memory up to that time: thousands of people filed by the casket, and the procession to Mount St. Mary's Cemetery contained hundreds of automobiles, among them that of Pendergast. Larsen and Hulston, *Pendergast!* 114–16.

Chapter Three

1. The liner arrived in New York that day.

2. The railroad attached two private cars to a regular train.

3. The first ward with a population of 19,923 cast 20,687 votes. In the second ward with a population of 18,478 there were 21,242 voters. The estimate was that in 1936 the machine voted sixty thousand "pads," or cemetery and other names.

4. O'Malley may not have been Pendergast's closest friend, although he

was a longtime associate. The Kansas City water department was corrupt to the core, and after Pendergast's fall it became evident that large sums of money paid out for discovery of water leaks, which then were fixed by employees of the department, went almost in entirety to the machine. See chap. 18.

Chapter Four

1. The number of out-of-state insurance companies totaled 137. Within the state there were 77 more. Companies operating only within the state, some of them associated with fraternal orders such as Woodmen of the World, Odd Fellows, and Maccabees, were subject to state courts, but the latter followed the decisions of the federal courts. William T. Kemper, Sr., was chairman of the Commerce Trust Company and the city's most prominent banker.

2. Robert J. Folonie was a partner in the leading firm of fire insurance attorneys in the United States, a Chicago firm, Hicks and Folonie.

3. A further sum, totaling $2 million, was impounded from excess premiums charged by companies operating only within Missouri.

4. Not long after Governor Stark took office his relations with Pendergast, hitherto excellent, for the machine had supported Stark, began to decline. By early summer they were poor, and when the governor took a cruise to Alaska, Pendergast asked him to stop off upon return in Colorado Springs for a conference. The boss was staying at the Broadmoor Hotel. At the meeting the name of O'Malley came up, and Pendergast asked Stark to continue the insurance commissioner in office for another four-year term (O'Malley had been appointed by Park in 1933). The boss seemed strangely sensitive about O'Malley, an unpopular figure as insurance commissioner because he had criticized the insurance programs of the fraternal orders. The governor told Pendergast that O'Malley's days were numbered but he could remain for a while as a holdover, depending upon good behavior. When the issue of the insurance compromise came before the state supreme court, over its acceptance for companies operating within the state, the governor told O'Malley not to argue for the compromise. O'Malley defied the governor, who fired him.

Chapter Five

1. This paragraph might seem elliptical, but the reader must bear in mind that the Chicago agent at this point had nothing more to go on, other than suspicion; there had been no investigation. A return for 1936 would be due March 15, 1937, and Street had a year thereafter, until March 15, 1938, to amend it.

2. Hartmann was not concerned with who tipped off Governor Stark, or why, the tip-off mentioned in the Introduction, but it is fairly clear that

when the official of the Bureau of Internal Revenue in Washington, who was from Missouri, resigned to take employment in New York, he acted for several reasons. He was irritated, probably angry, at bureau inaction, and perhaps felt its cause was the political alliance of Pendergast with the Roosevelt administration. He realized that Street's death meant the virtual end of the possibility of investigation, unless the bureau displayed more activity than it thus far had shown. And with the New York job in hand, he was under no compulsion to be discreet.

Chapter Six

1. The chronology here is unclear, as Hartmann could only relate when he came into the case. Maurice Milligan's *Missouri Waltz*, 172–73, tells of a visit by himself and Governor Stark early in the year, caused by the telephone call from the Washington reporter of the *Kansas City Star*. That summer of 1938, Stark and Milligan again visited Washington, and this is the visit to which Hartmann refers.

2. The above paragraph is confusing, and has explanation below. In dealing with the larger insurance companies Street held two meetings, one in May 1935, the other in March 1936. In both he made assessments, explaining at the time of the second meeting that the assembled executives should subtract the first assessment from the second.

3. For Fire Insurance Company of Philadelphia read: Fire Association of Philadelphia.

4. By "mere conclusion" the author evidently means a hunch or snap judgment or something without proof.

Chapter Seven

1. Evidently the year 1929 was not the year of purchase of the house and hence was a typographical error. Using the touch system, a typist easily could have touched a "9" instead of a "1," meaning that the year of purchase probably was 1921.

2. Doubtless Hartmann and his two assistants saw the possibility of disbarring McCormack, a point of leverage.

3. The present-day Hilton, on Michigan Avenue, is the former Stevens.

4. As older readers will know, photostatting was the duplicating process at that time; xeroxing did not become available until the 1960s.

Chapter Eight

1. As mentioned, there was no special train. The operation for a colostomy was performed at Menorah.

2. According to the Fourth Amendment, "The right of the people to be

secure in their persons, houses, papers, and effects, against unreasonable searches and seizures, shall not be violated, and no warrants shall issue but upon probable cause, supported by oath or affirmation, and particularly describing the place to be searched, and the persons or things to be seized."

3. Clay County, to the north of Jackson County (Kansas City), adjoined Platte County to the west, the location of the Pendergast track.

Chapter Nine

1. Raising of the bribe to $750,000 came to nothing; Pendergast, O'Malley, and McCormack received $460,000. This included a payment to Pendergast of $10,000.

2. Given medical costs of the 1930s this sum surely was for other purposes.

Chapter Ten

1. A distinguished Kansas City lawyer comments on Hartmann's statement that the maid read the letters out of curiosity: "If you can believe that, I have some swampland to sell you in Florida. Obviously, the treasury, FBI, or somebody paid the maid to remove the mail, and deliver it to the Feds for perusal so that they could know what O'Malley was up to."

2. "O'Neil" evidently was not McCormack, for the latter would have been "our friend over East" in St. Louis.

3. "Al" was A. L. McCormack. The lawyer mentioned in note 1 writes concerning Mrs. O'Malley: "More than once in the quoted portions of those letters she regrets that her husband's co-conspirator, Mr. McCormack, happened to find Forest Hanna as his attorney. The unspoken part of this is that Hanna was an honest lawyer, who actually advised McCormack in the light of McCormack's interests, rather than those of T. J. Pendergast. The Hanna name remains highly reputed in this community, and his son is now an appeals court judge on the Kansas City Court of Appeals, appointed to that position by [Governor] John Ashcroft."

4. Pendergast was becoming bitter over McCormack's talking.

5. "Haide" evidently was Paul L. Haid, president of the Insurance Executives Association of New York.

6. Truman had been in Jefferson City speaking to the legislature on good government, and, at President Roosevelt's insistence, communicated by both Farley and the president's press secretary, Stephen T. Early, flew back to Washington in a dangerous night flight, during a snowstorm, to cast the deciding vote on the Reorganization bill. Furious with the president for demanding his vote on a bill that he did not believe was worth a "tinker's damn," he called Early and told him to tell Roosevelt he did not

like to be treated like an office boy. He spoke with Early on Wednesday, March 22. The senator saw the president the next day, and the conversation was very uneasy. As was his wont, FDR showed friendship for the Missouri senator, and interspersed his concern and goodwill with the commentaries he intended to make. He thanked Truman for his contribution to the important bill that passed the Senate because of Truman's vote. But throughout the conversation he showed detailed knowledge of what was going on in Kansas City. He mentioned a visit to Washington of Police Director Otto P. Higgins. He inquired after Pendergast's health, which Truman assured him was excellent. He bluntly stated that he intended to clean up Kansas City politics. To be sure, during this confrontation Truman could not possibly have done anything for Pendergast, even if he had wished.

7. Pendergast's nephew Jim was flying to Washington to see Postmaster General Farley. As mentioned in the Introduction, the nephew in Truman's presence asked Farley to intervene in the investigation of his uncle.

8. Roy McKittrick was attorney general of the State of Missouri. The state as well as the federal government was involved in the Pendergast bribe because insurance companies operating only within Missouri also had had premiums impounded. The state supreme court had refused to accept the O'Malley arrangement for a division of those premiums, totaling $2 million.

9. Paul V. Barnett was a Kansas City lawyer. See note 12.

10. John T. Barker represented the State of Missouri in negotiation with the insurance companies. See his *Missouri Lawyer*.

11. "Al" here means A-l.

12. "J. A." was James P. Aylward; see chap. 2, note 7. Barnett attracted O'Malley because as a federal master he had issued a report favorable to the insurance companies.

13. R. R. Brewster was a Republican leader in Kansas City and a friend of the two federal district judges, Reeves and Otis. He received a retainer from Pendergast of $100,000, then an unheard-of fee locally. Larsen and Hulston, *Pendergast!* 143–44. John G. Madden was the boss's other lawyer.

14. See note 1.

Chapter Eleven

1. The Intelligence Unit of the Bureau of Internal Revenue, in the person of its chief, Elmer Irey, together with the commissioner of internal revenue, Guy T. Helvering, had pleaded with Attorney General Frank Murphy to delay the initial indictment, but Murphy flatly refused. The Treasury Department desired to include the failure of Pendergast to pay income on his businesses. Apparently Murphy desired credit for the investigation. He and the director of the Federal Bureau of Investigation, J. Edgar Hoover, made a trip to Kansas City on April 4, 1939. See Sidney Fine, *Frank Murphy: The Washington Years*.

Chapter Twelve

1. Pendergast served a year and a day, released early because of good behavior.

2. The out-of-state companies had to repay the entire sums awarded them. In addition, the State of Missouri assessed fines. For the latter see Appendix.

3. They were not carried out.

Chapter Thirteen

1. "Nolle prosequi"—L., unwilling to prosecute.

2. Carrollo was deported to Sicily.

Chapter Fourteen

1. In the 1930s each of the 114 counties of Missouri possessed a county court, an elective body of two judges and a presiding judge. The judges were in effect county commissioners, supervising county finances including road construction and eleemosynary institutions.

2. John W. Madden should not be confused with John G. Madden, one of Pendergast's lawyers in 1939.

Chapter Fifteen

1. The mayor was Bryce B. Smith.

2. In 1967, Halvorson made an oral history for the Harry S. Truman Library, testifying to an association with the later president in a savings and loan venture during the 1920s. Truman had organized a partnership with three individuals, one of whom was Halvorson, to sell stock—savings accounts. Halvorson and Truman later dropped out of the company. Ferrell, *Harry S. Truman*, 104–5.

Chapter Sixteen

1. Of all the explanations in the present book, Hartmann's account of Higgins is the most uncertain. One cannot see what, if anything, Higgins had on Schneider, apart presumably from the police director's vicelike hold on his department and his close connection with Carrollo who could act as an enforcer. Hartmann apparently knew no more than anyone else as to whether Schneider jumped from Fairfax Bridge or was pushed.

Chapter Seventeen

1. Gargotta was firing at Sheriff Bash, and surrendered when he ran out of ammunition.
2. According to Kansas City legend, Pendergast himself had gotten into a barroom fight with Fireman Jim Flynn, who lost. Admittedly Jim was drunk, or at least not sober.
3. The tax refers to the Social Security Act of 1935.

Chapter Eighteen

1. The ordinarily accurate Hartmann might seem to contradict himself by relating that Rathford had only one employee, Higinbotham, when he stated earlier that the firm had two or three employees. This may mean that over the years there were different employees.
2. As the preceding chapter relates, J. J. Pryor entered Leavenworth on January 20, 1940. Apart from its usefulness as a device to siphon money out of the water department, the Rathford Engineering Company possessed special political value. In 1932 the owner of a large wholesale chemical plant in the city, Matthew Thompson, offered a reward of $1,000 to anyone who would stand up to the machine. Not long afterward, two men from the department arrived at his office and told him there was a water leak nearby. Men began digging in front of the plant, and at the end of a few days had dug a ditch completely around the plant. No traffic could get in or out, and the men had shut off the water. Thompson withdrew his offer and the next day the men filled the ditch, turned on the water, and departed. John Joseph Fennelly, "Kansas City: 1925 to 1951," 27.

Chapter Nineteen

1. The WPA situation in Missouri was complicated, and Murray did not really control it until two or three years after he became state director. It is true that any applicant for employment needed endorsement of the Jackson County organization. But for the initial years commencing in 1935 the assistant director, a close friend of the state's junior senator, Truman, was in charge—Harry Easley, a banker in Webb City. Eventually Easley found the pressure from the organization too much; he was being asked to allot projects and money without knowing their purposes. At that juncture he resigned and returned to management of his bank.

Chapter Twenty

1. Years earlier, in 1918, Judge Reeves had had personal experience with vote fraud. He ran for Congress that year and was defeated by 12,000

votes; he lost one precinct by a vote of 700 to 1, although in that precinct only 30 people voted up to the time the polls closed. Appointed to the federal bench by President Warren G. Harding, Reeves was a Baptist Sunday school teacher, stern and austere. When after the vote frauds in the presidential election of 1936 he impaneled a grand jury, he did so under an old post–Civil War statute that allowed federal intervention in local elections in cases where citizens—it had been designed to protect blacks from the Ku Klux Klan—were denied the franchise or otherwise misrepresented at the polls. To be sure of impartiality he chose the jurors from outside Kansas City. He did so again in 1939.

2. Born on a Missouri farm, a devotee of the classics and the Bible, graduate of the law department of the University of Missouri, Judge Otis had been appointed to the federal bench in 1925 by President Calvin Coolidge.

Chapter Twenty-One

1. The machine's hold on the city was not as all-encompassing. To the south, in the wealthy precincts, control was never as secure as in the first and second wards, Alderman Jim's enclave next to the Missouri River. The machine did, of course, control the city government.

2. The new director of police in Kansas City, a disciple of J. Edgar Hoover, was Lear B. Reed. He introduced all the techniques of the Federal Bureau of Investigation.

Further Reading

Adler, Frank J. *Roots in a Moving Stream: The Centennial History of Congregation B'nai Jehudah of Kansas City, 1870–1970.* Kansas City: The Congregation, 1972.

Anon. "The Governor of Missouri Helps Indict the Boss of Kansas City and Becomes a Presidential Possibility." *Life* 6, no. 17 (April 24, 1939): 15–19.

Barker, John T. *Missouri Lawyer.* Philadelphia: Dorrance, 1949.

Beatty, Jerome. "A Political Boss Talks about His Job." *American* 115 (February 1933): 30–31, 108–9.

Brown, A[ndrew] Theodore. *The Politics of Reform: Kansas City's Municipal Government, 1925–1930.* Kansas City: Community Studies, 1958.

Coghlan, Ralph. "Boss Pendergast: King of Kansas City, Emperor of Missouri." *Forum and Century* 97 (January–June 1937): 67–72.

Dorsett, Lyle W. *Franklin D. Roosevelt and the City Bosses.* Port Washington, N.Y.: Kennikat, 1977.

———. *The Pendergast Machine.* New York: Oxford University Press, 1958.

———. "Truman and the Pendergast Machine." *Midcontinent American Studies Journal* 7 (1966): 16–27.

Dunar, Andrew J. *The Truman Scandals and the Politics of Morality.* Columbia: University of Missouri Press, 1984.

Evans, Timothy E. " 'This Certainly Is Relief!': Matthew S. Murray and Missouri Politics during the Depression." *Missouri Historical Society Bulletin* 28 (July 1972): 219–33.

Farley, James A. *Jim Farley's Story: The Roosevelt Years.* New York: McGraw-Hill, 1948.

Fennelly, John Joseph. "Kansas City: 1925 to 1951." Senior thesis, Princeton University, 1952.

Ferrell, Robert H. *Harry S. Truman: A Life.* Columbia: University of Missouri Press, 1994.

Fine, Sidney. *Frank Murphy: The Washington Years.* Ann Arbor: University of Michigan Press, 1984.

Gosnell, Harold F. *Machine Politics: Chicago Model.* Chicago: University of Chicago Press, 1937.

Hamby, Alonzo L. *Man of the People: A Life of Harry S. Truman.* New York: Oxford University Press, 1995.

Irey, Elmer L., and William J. Slocum. "How We Smashed the Pendergast Machine." *Coronet* 23 (December 1947): 67–76.

———. *The Tax Dodgers: The Inside Story of the T-Men's War with America's Political and Underworld Hoodlums.* New York: Greenberg, 1948.

Kelley, Herbert. "Youth Goes into Action." *American* 119 (February 1935): 12–13, 110–12.

Kirkendall, Richard S. *A History of Missouri: 1919 to 1953.* Columbia: University of Missouri Press, 1986.

———. "Truman and the Pendergast Machine: A Comment." *Midcontinent American Studies Journal* 7 (1966): 36–39.

Larsen, Lawrence H. *Federal Justice in Western Missouri: The Judges, the Cases, the Times.* Columbia: University of Missouri Press, 1994.

———. "A Political Boss at Bay: Thomas J. Pendergast in Federal Prison, 1939–1940." *Missouri Historical Review* 86 (1991–1992): 396–417.

Larsen, Lawrence H., and Nancy J. Hulston. *Pendergast!* Columbia: University of Missouri Press, 1997.

———. "Criminal Aspects of the Pendergast Machine." *Missouri Historical Review* 91 (1996–1997): 168–80.

McCullough, David. *Truman.* New York: Simon and Schuster, 1992.

McCullough, Spencer R. " 'Boss' Pendergast Tells the Story of His Remarkable Career." *St. Louis Post-Dispatch,* September 12, 1937.

Maney, Patrick J. *The Roosevelt Presence: A Biography of Franklin Delano Roosevelt.* New York: Twayne, 1992.

Mason, Frank. *Truman and the Pendergasts.* Evanston, Ill.: Regency, 1963.

Mayerberg, Samuel S. *Chronicle of an American Crusader: Alumni Lectures Delivered at the Hebrew Union College, Cincinnati, Ohio, December 7–10, 1942.* New York: Bloch, 1944.

Messick, Hank. *Secret File.* New York: Putnam's, 1969.

Miller, Richard Lawrence. *Truman: The Rise to Power.* New York: McGraw-Hill, 1986.

Miller, William D. *Mr. Crump of Memphis.* Baton Rouge: Louisiana State University Press, 1964.

Milligan, Maurice. *Missouri Waltz: The Inside Story of the Pendergast Machine.* New York: Scribner, 1948.

Mitchell, Franklin D. *Embattled Democracy: Missouri Democratic Politics, 1919–1932.* Columbia: University of Missouri Press, 1968.

Otis, Merrill E. *In the Day's Work of a Federal Judge: A Miscellany of Opinions, Addresses and Extracts from Opinions and Addresses.* Kansas City: Brown-White, 1937.

Powell, Eugene James. *Tom's Boy Harry: The First Complete, Authentic Story of Harry Truman's Connection with the Pendergast Machine.* Jefferson City, Mo.: Hawthorn, 1948.

Reddig, William M. *Tom's Town: Kansas City and the Pendergast Legend.* Philadelphia: Lippincott, 1947.

Reed, Lear B. *Human Wolves: Seventeen Years of War on Crime.* Kansas City: Brown-White-Lowell, 1941.

Royko, Mike. *Boss: Richard J. Daley of Chicago.* New York: Dutton, 1973.

Salter, J. T. *Boss Rule: Portraits in City Politics.* New York: McGraw-Hill, 1935.

Schauffler, Edward R. "The End of Pendergast." *Forum* 102 (July 1939): 18–23.

Schmidtlein, Gene. "Harry S. Truman and the Pendergast Machine." *Midcontinent American Studies Journal* 2 (1966): 28–35.

Slavens, George Everett. "Lloyd C. Stark as a Political Reformer: 1936–1941." Master's thesis, University of Missouri, Columbia, 1957.

Spiering, Frank. *The Man Who Got Capone.* Indianapolis: Bobbs-Merrill, 1976.

Walsh, Jerome. "A Special Book Review." *Kansas City Bar Bulletin* (May 1948): 12a–d.

Where These Rocky Bluffs Meet: Including the Story of the Kansas City

Ten-Year Plan, with Illustrations. Kansas City: Chamber of Commerce, 1938.

Williams, T. Harry. *Huey Long.* New York: Knopf, 1969.

Zink, Harold. *City Bosses in the United States: A Study of Twenty Municipal Bosses.* Durham, N.C.: Duke University Press, 1930.

Index

Abry, Philip, 100–101
American House (Kansas City), 173
Anthon, Ferris J., 14
Aylward, James P., 96

Baker, A. R., 155
Balkema, P. R., 60–61
Barker, J. T., 30, 95
Barnett, Paul V., 27, 95–96, 179
Bash, Thomas B., 14
Beach, Harry D., 17–19, 23
Berkshire Arms Hotel (Kansas City), 18
Berry, Charles O'B., 67, 121
Binaggia, Rocco, 108
Binagio, Dominick, 106
B'nai Jehudah (Kansas City temple), 174
Board of Tax Appeals, U.S., 49, 67
Boatwright, William G., 103
Boyle, William D., 142–45, 149–52
Boyle-Pryor Construction Company, 146, 149, 154, 156–57
Brennan, "Boots," 95
Brewster, R. R., 96, 102–3, 179
Brinks Express Company, 144–45
Broderick, William S., 63–64
Buford, Anthony, 93
Bureau of Internal Revenue. *See* Internal Revenue Bureau
Burnett, William J., 150

Capone, Alphonse, 5, 55
Carey, Maurice, 128
Carroll, James E., 68–69, 93–95

Carrollo, Charles V., 21, 23–25, 67, 98–99, 105–12, 118, 133–34, 139, 160–61, 164, 166
Carrollo, Frank (brother), 108
Carrollo, Samuel (brother), 108
Catholic Church, 173
Centropolis Crusher Company, 13, 66
Charles L. Crane Agency, 50–51, 55
Christian Brothers College High School (St. Joseph), 11
Chronicle of an American Crusader (Mayerberg), 174
City Manager's Emergency Fund, 124–25, 140
City National Bank and Trust Company (Chicago), 37, 40, 42, 45–46, 48, 50, 53, 91–92, 129–30
Civil Aeronautics Commission, 90
Claiborne, Leonard L., 14
Clark, Bennett Champ, 3, 8–9
Clough, Arthur M., 121
Cohen, Harry, 60
Collet, John Caskie, 139, 153
Collyer's Eye (newspaper), 60
Commerce Trust Company (Kansas City), 63, 65
Congress. *See* House of Representatives; Senate
Congress Hotel (Chicago), 56, 70
Constitution, U.S., 107, 137, 164
Coronado Hotel (St. Louis), 68–72
Cosgrove, John, 94
Cowboy Inn (Kansas City), 108–9
Cross, Adaline A., 90–92